Kaplan Publishing are constantly finding nev
looking for exam success and our online res
extra dimension to your studies.

CW00983723

This book comes with free MyKaplan online
study anytime, anywhere. **This free online resource is not sold separately and is included in the price of the book.**

Having purchased this book, you have access to the following online study materials:

CONTENT	AAT	
	Text	Kit
Electronic version of the book	✓	✓
Knowledge Check tests with instant answers	✓	
Mock assessments online	✓	✓
Material updates	✓	✓

How to access your online resources

Received this book as part of your Kaplan course?
If you have a MyKaplan account, your full online resources will be added automatically, in line with the information in your course confirmation email. If you've not used MyKaplan before, you'll be sent an activation email once your resources are ready.

Bought your book from Kaplan?
We'll automatically add your online resources to your MyKaplan account. If you've not used MyKaplan before, you'll be sent an activation email.

Bought your book from elsewhere?
Go to **www.mykaplan.co.uk/add-online-resources**
Enter the ISBN number found on the title page and back cover of this book.
Add the unique pass key number contained in the scratch panel below.
You may be required to enter additional information during this process to set up or confirm your account details.

This code can only be used once for the registration of this book online. This registration and your online content will expire when the examinations covered by this book have taken place. Please allow one hour from the time you submit your book details for us to process your request.

Please scratch the film to access your unique code.

Please be aware that this code is case-sensitive and you will need to include the dashes within the passcode, but not when entering the ISBN.

KAPLAN

PUBLISHING

AAT

Q2022

THE BUSINESS ENVIRONMENT

Synoptic Assessment

EXAM KIT

This Exam Kit supports study for the following AAT qualifications:
AAT Level 2 Certificate in Accounting
AAT Level 2 Certificate in Bookkeeping
AAT Certificate in Accounting at SCQF Level 6

British Library Cataloguing-in-Publication Data

A catalogue record for this book is available from the British Library.

Published by:

Kaplan Publishing UK

Unit 2 The Business Centre

Molly Millar's Lane

Wokingham

Berkshire

RG41 2QZ

ISBN: 978-1-83996-583-8

© Kaplan Financial Limited, 2023

Printed and bound in Great Britain.

CONTENTS

	Page
Synoptic assessment specification	P.4
Unit specific information	P.5
Assessment objectives	P.7
Index to questions and answers	P.9
Exam technique	P.10
Kaplan's recommended revision approach	P.11
The Kaplan Revision Plan	P.12

Practice questions	1
Answers to practice questions	155
Mock assessment questions	243
Mock assessment answers	259

Features in this exam kit

In addition to providing a wide ranging bank of real exam style questions, we have also included in this kit:

- unit-specific information and advice on exam technique

- our recommended approach to make your revision for this particular unit as effective as possible.

You will find a wealth of other resources to help you with your studies on the AAT website:

www.aat.org.uk/

Quality and accuracy are of the utmost importance to us so if you spot an error in any of our products, please send an email to mykaplanreporting@kaplan.com with full details, or follow the link to the feedback form in MyKaplan.

Our Quality Co-ordinator will work with our technical team to verify the error and take action to ensure it is corrected in future editions.

SYNOPTIC ASSESSMENT SPECIFICATION

AAT Q2022 Business Environment Synoptic Assessment is an assessment which students must complete if they are to achieve the appropriate qualification upon completion of a qualification. In the case of the Level 2 Certificate in Accounting, students must pass all of the mandatory assessments and the synoptic assessment to achieve the qualification.

As a Synoptic Assessment is attempted following completion of individual units, it draws upon knowledge and understanding from those units. It may be appropriate for students to retain their study materials for individual units until they have successfully completed the synoptic assessment for that qualification.

All units within the Level 2 Certificate in Accounting are mandatory. Three units are assessed individually in end of unit assessments, but this qualification also includes a synoptic assessment, sat towards the end of the qualification, which draws on and assesses knowledge and understanding from across the qualification.

- Introduction to Bookkeeping – end of unit assessment

- Principles of Bookkeeping Controls – end of unit assessment

- Principles of Costing – end of unit assessment

- The Business Environment – assessed within the synoptic assessment only

Note that Principles of Costing is a unit assessment only and is not assessed as part of the synoptic assessment. Note also that The Business Environment is assessed in the synoptic assessment only.

Summary of learning outcomes from underlying units which are assessed in the synoptic assessment

Underlying unit	Learning outcomes required
The Business Environment	LO1, LO2, LO3, LO4, LO5, LO6, LO7
Introduction to Bookkeeping	LO1, LO2, LO3
Principles of Bookkeeping Controls	LO1, LO2, LO3

UNIT SPECIFIC INFORMATION

THE EXAM

FORMAT OF THE ASSESSMENT

The specimen synoptic assessment comprises eight tasks and covers all eight assessment objectives. Students will be assessed by computer-based assessment. Marking of the assessment is partially by computer and partially human marked.

In any one assessment, students may not be assessed on all content, or on the full depth or breadth of a piece of content. The content assessed may change over time to ensure validity of assessment, but all assessment criteria will be tested over time.

The synoptic assessment will ask students to apply knowledge and skills gained across the qualification in an integrated way, within a workplace context. Scenarios will change over time to ensure the validity of the assessment.

The following weighting is based upon the AAT Qualification Specification documentation which may be subject to variation.

	Assessment objective	Weighting
AO1	Demonstrate an understanding of the different business types and their functions	10%
AO2	Demonstrate an understanding of the finance function, its information requirements and sources, and its role in the wider organisation	13%
AO3	Demonstrate an understanding of corporate social responsibility (CSR), ethics and sustainability	14%
AO4	Process bookkeeping transactions and communicate information	22%
A05	Produce and reconcile control accounts and use journals to correct errors	10%
A06	Demonstrate an understanding of the principles of contract law	7%
A07	Demonstrate an understanding of bookkeeping systems, receipts and payments, and the importance of information and data security	10%
A08	Demonstrate an understanding of the global business environment	14%
	Total	100%

Time allowed

2 hours

PASS MARK

The pass mark for all AAT assessments is 70%.

 Always keep your eye on the clock and make sure you attempt all questions!

DETAILED SYLLABUS

The detailed syllabus and study guide written by the AAT can be found at:

www.aat.org.uk/

DETAILED SYLLABUS

ASSESSMENT OBJECTIVES

To perform this synoptic assessment effectively you will need to know and understand the following:

Assessment objective 1	Demonstrate an understanding of the different business types and their functions
Related learning outcomes	**The Business Environment** LO4 Understand the impact of setting up different types of business entity LO5 Understand the finance function within an organisation
Assessment objective 2	Demonstrate an understanding of the finance function, its information requirements and sources, and its role in the wider organisation
Related learning outcomes	**The Business Environment** LO5 Understand the finance function within an organisation LO6 Produce work in appropriate formats and communicate effectively LO7 Understand the importance of information to business operations
Assessment objective 3	Demonstrate an understanding of corporate social responsibility (CSR), ethics and sustainability
Related learning outcomes	**The Business Environment** LO3 Understand key principles of corporate social responsibility (CSR), ethics and sustainability
Assessment objective 4	Process bookkeeping transactions and communicate information
Related learning outcome	**Introduction to Bookkeeping** LO1 Understand how to set up bookkeeping systems LO2 Process customer transactions LO3 Produce supplier transactions **The Business Environment** LO6 Produce work in appropriate formats and communicate effectively
Assessment objective 5	Produce and reconcile control accounts and use journals to correct errors
	Principles of Bookkeeping Controls LO1 Use control accounts LO2 Reconcile a bank statement with the cash book LO3 Use the journal

Assessment objective 6	Demonstrate an understanding of the principles of contract law
	The Business Environment LO1 Understand the principles of contract law
Assessment objective 7	Demonstrate an understanding of bookkeeping systems, receipts and payments, and the importance of information and data security
	The Business Environment LO7 Understand the importance of information to business operations **Introduction to Bookkeeping** LO1 Understand how to set up bookkeeping systems LO2 Process customer transactions LO3 Produce supplier transactions **Principles of Bookkeeping Controls** LO1 Use control accounts LO2 Reconcile a bank statement with the cash book LO3 Use the journal
Assessment objective 8	Demonstrate an understanding of the global business environment
	The Business Environment LO2 Understand the external business environment

P.8

KAPLAN PUBLISHING

INDEX TO QUESTIONS AND ANSWERS

		Page number	
		Question	Answer
THE BUSINESS ENVIRONMENT			
1 – 15	LO1 Understand the principles of contract law	1	155
16 – 30	LO2 Understand the external business environment	5	158
31 – 45	LO3 Understand the key principles of CSR, ethics and sustainability	9	160
46 – 60	LO4 Understand the impact of setting up different types of business entity	14	163
61 – 75	LO5 Understand the finance function within an organisation	19	166
76 – 90	LO6 Produce work in appropriate formats and communicate effectively	24	169
91 – 105	LO7 Understand the importance of information to business operations	30	173
INTRODUCTION TO BOOKKEEPING			
106 – 124	LO1 Understand how to set up bookkeeping systems	35	177
125 – 139	LO2 Process customer transactions	51	187
140 – 159	LO3 Process supplier transactions	66	196
PRINCIPLES OF BOOKKEEPING CONTROLS			
160 – 171	LO1 Use control accounts	91	207
172 – 191	LO2 Reconcile a bank statement with the cash book	105	216
192 – 236	LO3 Use the journal	127	226

EXAM TECHNIQUE

- **Do not skip any of the material** in the syllabus.

- **Read each question** *very* carefully.

- **Double-check your answer** before committing yourself to it.

- Answer **every** question – if you do not know an answer to a multiple choice question or true/false question, you don't lose anything by guessing. Think carefully before you **guess**.

- If you are answering a multiple-choice question, **eliminate first those answers that you know are wrong.** Then choose the most appropriate answer from those that are left.

- **Don't panic** if you realise you've answered a question incorrectly. Getting one question wrong will not mean the difference between passing and failing.

Computer-based exams – tips

- Do not attempt a CBA until you have **completed all study material** relating to it.

- On the AAT website there is a CBA demonstration. It is **ESSENTIAL** that you attempt this before your real CBA. You will become familiar with how to move around the CBA screens and the way that questions are formatted, increasing your confidence and speed in the actual exam.

- Be sure you understand how to use the **software** before you start the exam. If in doubt, ask the assessment centre staff to explain it to you.

- Questions are **displayed on the screen** and answers are entered using keyboard and mouse. At the end of the exam, in the case of those units not subject to human marking, you are given a certificate showing the result you have achieved.

- In addition to the traditional multiple-choice question type, CBAs will also contain **other types of questions**, such as number entry questions, drag and drop, true/false, pick lists or drop down menus or hybrids of these.

- In some CBAs you will have to type in complete computations or written answers.

- You need to be sure you **know how to answer questions** of this type before you sit the exam, through practice.

KAPLAN'S RECOMMENDED REVISION APPROACH

QUESTION PRACTICE IS THE KEY TO SUCCESS

Success in professional examinations relies upon you acquiring a firm grasp of the required knowledge at the tuition phase. In order to be able to do the questions, knowledge is essential.

However, the difference between success and failure often hinges on your exam technique on the day and making the most of the revision phase of your studies.

The **Kaplan Study Text** is the starting point, designed to provide the underpinning knowledge to tackle all questions. However, in the revision phase, poring over text books is not the answer.

Kaplan Pocket Notes are designed to help you quickly revise a topic area; however you then need to practise questions. There is a need to progress to exam style questions as soon as possible, and to tie your exam technique and technical knowledge together.

The importance of question practice cannot be over-emphasised.

The recommended approach below is designed by expert tutors in the field, in conjunction with their knowledge of the examiner and the specimen assessment.

You need to practise as many questions as possible in the time you have left.

OUR AIM

Our aim is to get you to the stage where you can attempt exam questions confidently, to time, in a closed book environment, with no supplementary help (i.e. to simulate the real examination experience).

Practising your exam technique is also vitally important for you to assess your progress and identify areas of weakness that may need more attention in the final run up to the examination.

In order to achieve this we recognise that initially you may feel the need to practice some questions with open book help.

Good exam technique is vital.

THE KAPLAN REVISION PLAN

Stage 1: Assess areas of strengths and weaknesses

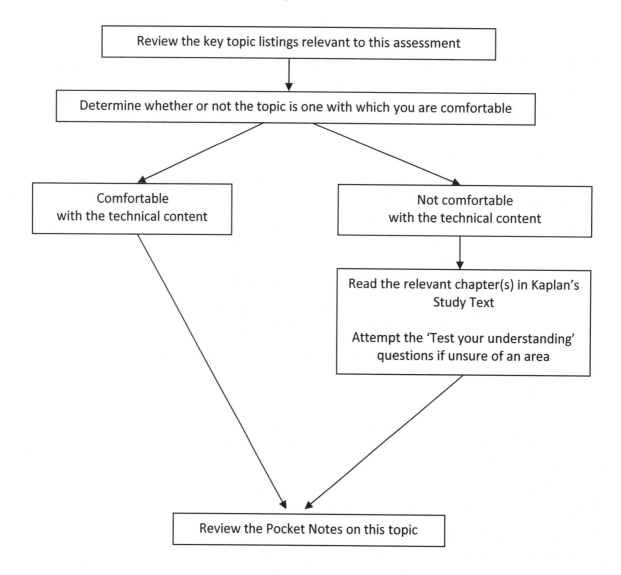

Stage 2: Practice questions

Follow the order of revision of topics as presented in this Kit and attempt the questions in the order suggested.

Try to avoid referring to Study Texts and your notes and the model answer until you have completed your attempt.

Review your attempt with the model answer and assess how much of the answer you achieved.

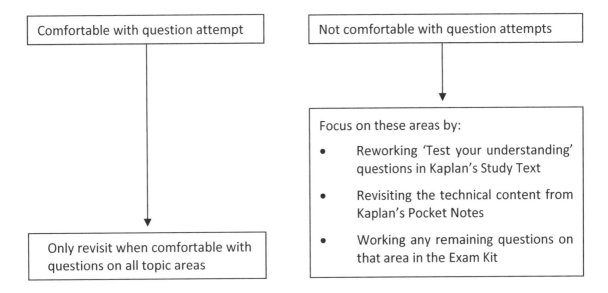

| Comfortable with question attempt | Not comfortable with question attempts |

Focus on these areas by:

- Reworking 'Test your understanding' questions in Kaplan's Study Text
- Revisiting the technical content from Kaplan's Pocket Notes
- Working any remaining questions on that area in the Exam Kit

Only revisit when comfortable with questions on all topic areas

Stage 3: Final pre-exam revision

We recommend that you **attempt at least one mock examination** containing a set of previously unseen exam-standard questions.

Attempt the mock CBA online in timed, closed book conditions to simulate the real exam experience.

Section 1

PRACTICE QUESTIONS

THE BUSINESS ENVIRONMENT

LO1 UNDERSTAND THE PRINCIPLES OF CONTRACT LAW

1   COMMON LAW

Which of the following TWO statements regarding 'common law' are NOT correct?

A   It is the body of law as made by judges through the determination of cases

B   It is law created by Parliament

C   It is the system of law that emerged following the Norman Conquest in 1066

D   In the event of conflict with equity the common law will prevail

2   CIVIL LAW

Identify whether the following statements regarding civil law are true or false.

	True	False
It is the body of laws that does not relate to criminal offences		
It is law created by judges through decisions made in cases		

3   CASE LAW I

Identify whether the following statements regarding case law are true or false.

	True	False
The final court of appeal in England and Wales is the Supreme Court		
'Obiter dicta' is the part of the legal judgement that establishes the precedent that is to be binding on lower courts		

4   CASE LAW II

Identify whether the following statements regarding case law are true or false.

	True	False
Common law developed from local customs		
The Supreme Court can be bound by decisions of the Court of Appeal		

5   OFFER AND ACCEPTANCE

An offer was made by A to sell goods on the 1st April for £2,000. B the offeree telephoned A on the 5th April offering to pay £1,800 for the goods.

On the 8th April, A offered to sell the goods to C for £1,900, and C accepted this offer on the same day. On the 7th April, B sent a letter to A which was received on the 10th April agreeing to pay the £2,000 asking price for the goods.

Which one of the following is correct?

A   There is a contract between A and B created on the 7th April

B   There is a contract between A and B created on the 10th April

C   There is a contract between A and C

D   There is no contract created

6   OFFER AND INVITATION TO TREAT

A coat was displayed in a shop window with a price tag attached which read £10. The price tag should have read £100. X who saw this went into the shop and demanded the coat for £10.

Which one of the following is correct?

A   As the window display is an offer X can demand the coat at £10.

B   The window display is merely an invitation to treat and the shopkeeper does not have to sell the coat to X.

C   The shopkeeper can refuse to sell the coat for £10, but cannot refuse to sell the coat to X for £100 if X was prepared to pay this sum.

D   The shopkeeper would be bound to sell the coat to any customer prepared to pay this £100.

7   CONSIDERATION I

All simple contracts must be supported by consideration from each party.

Identify whether the following statements are true or false.

	True	False
Consideration must be sufficient		
Past consideration is valid consideration		

8   CONSIDERATION II

Identify whether the following statements regarding consideration are true or false.

	True	False
Executory consideration is a promise to do something in the future after the contract is made		
Executed consideration is consideration that has been provided in the past		

9   REMEDIES FOR BREACH OF CONTRACT I

Identify whether the following statements regarding remedies for breach of contract are true or false.

	True	False
Damages are a common law remedy.		
Where a judge orders a defendant to perform their contractual obligations this is known as an 'injunction'.		

10   REMEDIES FOR BREACH OF CONTRACT II

Identify whether the following statements regarding remedies for breach of contract are true or false.

	True	False
A contract contains a term which states a fixed sum is payable in the event of breach. The sum is a genuine pre-estimate of the expected loss. This is an example of a 'penalty clause'.		
Adam has a contract with Colin. Four weeks prior to the agreed completion date, Colin telephones Adam out of courtesy to say he has double-booked and will be unable to carry out the work as agreed. This is an example of an 'express anticipatory breach of contract'		

11   COUNTER-OFFER

What is the principal effect of a counter-offer?

A   It destroys the original offer and replaces it with a new offer

B   It creates a binding contract based on the terms of the counter-offer

C   It creates a binding contract based on the terms of the original offer

D   It has no legal effect

12   SHOP WINDOW DISPLAY

George sees a television for sale in the window of a shop, with a sign attached stating 'LIMITED OFFER PRICE £50'

This is an example of which of the following?

A   An invitation to treat

B   A valid offer

C   A mere puff or boast

D   A statement of intention to sell

13   REVOCATION OF OFFER

Identify whether the following statements regarding revocation of an offer are true or false.

	True	False
Revocation of an offer must be made before the offer is accepted		
Revocation of an offer can be communicated by the offeror or any third party		

14   STANDARD OF PROOF

Identify whether the following statements regarding the standard of proof are true or false.

	True	False
The standard of proof required in a civil case is 'on the balance of probabilities		
The standard of proof required in a criminal case is 'beyond any doubt'		

15   DELEGATED LEGISLATION

Identify whether the following statements regarding delegated legislation are true or false.

	True	False
Statute and statutory instruments are both forms of delegated legislation		
Bye laws and orders in council are both forms of delegated legislation		

LO2 UNDERSTAND THE EXTERNAL BUSINESS ENVIRONMENT

16   INDIRECT TAXES

Which TWO of the taxes from the following list are indirect taxes?

A   Corporation tax

B   Value Added Tax (VAT)

C   Income tax

D   Import duties

17   PERSONAL TAXES

Which TWO of the following are taxes imposed on an individual, rather than a business?

A   Corporation tax

B   Import duties

C   Income tax

D   Capital gains tax

18   EXCHANGE RATES

Identify how the movement in the UK sterling exchange rate can be defined in each of the following examples.

Exchange rate movement	Choose from picklist
A movement in the exchange rate results in UK sterling buying fewer Euros than before	
A movement in the exchange rate results in UK sterling buying more Australian dollars than before	

Picklist: UK sterling has appreciated, UK sterling has depreciated

19   GOVERNMENT CONTROL

State whether each of the following statements is true or false.

Statement	True / False
An increase in interest rates will lead to an increase in demand for normal goods	
A reduction in tax rates will lead to an increase in demand for goods and services	
The annual rate of inflation in a country will always be constant from one year to the next	

20 TYPES OF TAX

Match the type of tax with the definition stated.

Definition	Type of tax
A tax which takes an increasing proportion of income as income increases	
A tax which takes a fixed proportion of income, irrespective of how high or low that income is	
A tax that takes an increasing proportion of income as it decreases	

Picklist: Progressive tax, proportional tax, regressive tax

21 CHARACTERISTICS OF A GOOD TAX

Identify which TWO items from the following list are characteristics of a good tax?

- Simple to understand
- Arbitrary
- Effective to maximise tax collected
- Convenient
- Fair

22 FISCAL POLICY

Which one of the following is the correct definition of fiscal policy?

A   Fiscal policy is the manner in which government chooses to spend cash

B   Fiscal policy is the manner of how a government chooses impose and collect taxes

C   Fiscal policy is the use of government spending to influence the economy

D   Fiscal policy is the use of taxation and government spending to influence the economy

23 INFERIOR GOODS

Which one of the following statements explains the demand for inferior goods?

A   Demand for inferior goods is unaffected by changes in income

B   Demand for inferior goods will rise as income falls

C   Demand for inferior goods will rise as income rises

D   Demand for inferior goods will remain unchanged when income rises

2

24   SUBSTITUTE GOODS

Identify whether each of the following statements relating to substitute goods is true or false.

Statement	Choose from picklist
If product A is regarded as a substitute for product B, and the price of product B falls, there will be less demand for product A	
If products D and E are regarded as substitutes for each other, an increase in the price of product E will result in increase in demand for both products	

Picklist: True, False

25   COMPLEMENTARY GOODS I

If products S and T are complementary goods, which one of the following statements is true?

A   If the price of product S falls, demand for product T will fall

B   If the price of product S rises, demand for product T will fall

C   If the price of product S rises, demand for product T will rise

D   If the price of product S rises, demand for product T will be unaffected

26   COMPLEMENTARY GOODS II

Which ONE of the following is a complementary product for a bicycle?

Statement	✓
A mobile phone	
A safety helmet	
A lightweight jacket	
A pair of training shoes	

27   INCOME EFFECT

Which of the following statements correctly explains the income effect relating to the demand for goods?

Statement	✓
If a supplier increases prices, consumers may switch to lower-priced products, leading to a fall in demand	
For expensive items, if a supplier increases prices, consumers may not be able to purchase the product, leading to a fall in demand	

28 MICROECONOMICS

Which one of the following statements correctly defines microeconomics?

Statement	✓
Microeconomics considers aggregate behaviour, producer and consumer behaviour and the workings of the economy as a whole	
Microeconomics considers the economic policies and activities of the government	
Microeconomics considers the economic behaviour and decisions of one industry only	
Microeconomics considers the economic behaviour of individual consumers, firms and industries	

29 INCOME TAX

The UK income tax system taxes individuals with a higher income at a higher rate that those with a lower income.

What type of tax is this?

A   An indirect tax

B   A proportional tax

C   A progressive tax

D   A regressive tax

30 BUSINESS TAXES

Identify which taxes are imposed on a sole trader and company (select all that apply)?

	Sole trader ✓	Company ✓
Corporation tax		
Import duties		
Income tax		

LO3 UNDERSTAND KEY PRINCIPLES OF CSR, ETHICS AND SUSTAINABILITY

31   PRINCIPLES

The fundamental code of ethics set out five principles that a professional accountant is required to comply with. Two principles are objectivity and professional competence/due care.

Select TWO other ethical principles from the list below.

A   Confidence

B   Integrity

C   Truthfulness

D   Confidentiality

32   COMPANY SHARES

Your father owns some shares in a company which your company audits. You have recently found out that the company is struggling. This is going to be announced publicly shortly and will have an adverse effect on the share price.

Which TWO fundamental ethical principles prevent you from telling your father about this?

A   Confidentiality

B   Objectivity

C   Professional Behaviour

D   Professional competence and due care

E   Integrity

33   TAX ADVICE

Your best friend has recently started up in business and really needs some tax advice. Because they know you are training to be an accountant they have automatically assumed you are the right person to give advice.

Which fundamental ethical principle prevents you from advising your best friend particularly regarding the fact that it is tax advice that he/she is seeking?

A   Confidentiality

B   Objectivity

C   Professional Behaviour

D   Professional competence and due care

E   Integrity

34   CLIENT DISCUSSION

You and a work colleague decide to go out for dinner after work. Whilst in the restaurant you start to discuss a client and the issues which this client is currently facing. Unbeknown to you the CEO of their major supplier is sat at the next table and hears everything which you have discussed.

Which fundamental ethical principle prevents you and your colleague from discussing this in public?

A   Confidentiality

B   Objectivity

C   Professional Behaviour

D   Professional competence and due care

E   Integrity

35   ACCOUNTING LEGISLATION

Your work colleague has decided not to comply with the relevant accounting legislation when preparing a client's account as they 'can't be bothered'.

Which TWO fundamental ethical principles is your colleague in breach of?

A   Confidentiality

B   Objectivity

C   Professional Behaviour

D   Professional competence and due care

E   Integrity

36   FRAUD

You have recently discovered that your manager is committing fraud. Your manager suspects that you know, and has threatened you with termination of your contract if you decide to whistle blow him.

Which threat to fundamental principles are you faced with?

A   Self Interest

B   Self Review

C   Familiarity

D   Advocacy

E   Intimidation

37   **NEW CLIENT**

Your company has recently taken on a new client and you have been asked to prepare the monthly management accounts. As soon as you start work on the accounts you realise that it is your aunt's company.

Which threat to principles are you faced with?

A   Self Interest

B   Self Review

C   Familiarity

D   Advocacy

E   Intimidation

38   **3 Ps**

What do the 3 Ps relate to in terms of balancing economic, environment and social needs?

A   People, Planet, Product

B   Planet, Place, Product

C   Profit, People, Planet

D   Price, People, Product

E   Profit, Place, People

39   **SUSTAINABLE**

Kapfin is looking to become more sustainable and a manager believes that she has come up with a few amazing suggestions.

Which ONE of these suggestions relates to sustainability?

A   Encourage all staff and students to use their own cars to travel to and from Kapfin.

B   Ensure all lights and computers are left on in the evening to prevent break-ins.

C   Encourage all students and staff to throw paper in the normal waste bin.

D   Encourage all Kapfin staff to work through their lunch.

E   To look into the possibility of providing the AAT textbook via e-books instead of providing a paper copy to students.

40   SUSTAINABILITY

Your friend is being encouraged to make a suggestion of how to improve sustainability within his/her workplace.

Which ONE of the following suggestions should he/she put forward to his/her manager?

A   Encourage all staff to print their work and maintain in lever arch files for audit trail purposes.

B   Look at installing motion sensor lights into the office block.

C   Encourage the Financial Accountant to replace his/her 2.0L Diesel BMW with a 3.5L Petrol BMW.

D   Suggest that all Monthly regional meetings should be done in the most central regional office instead of online.

E   Ensure all trainee accountants complete their CPD.

41   SOLAR PANELS

A company is trying to improve sustainability and it is considering installing solar panels on the office roof to reduce their yearly electricity costs. However, the initial costs of implementing this is 20% higher than originally budgeted for.

From a sustainability perspective, should the company still pursue this even though it is going to have an adverse impact on cost?

A   Yes

B   No.

42   CSR OBJECTIVES

Review each of the practical situations below, and match each situation with the appropriate corporate social responsibility (CSR) objective from the drop-down menu. You may use a CSR objective more than once if required.

Practical situation	CSR objective
Your organisation has a policy of encouraging all members of the finance department to study for an appropriate accountancy qualification and proving financial support for those who do so.	
Your organisation will shortly introduce 'paperless office' procedures whereby all customer orders are processed online and an accounting software package maintains the sales and purchase ledger accounts.	
Your organisation issues a "Corporate Policy of Ethical Practices" which it requires all potential suppliers to agree to before purchasing goods and services from them.	

Your organisation is currently installing lighting with movement sensors, so that lighting will automatically be switched off if no movement is sensed for 5 minutes. The lighting can be activated by movement only.	
Your organisation has a policy, wherever practicable, of permitting employees to work flexible hours, including working from home.	

Drop-down menu choices:

Environmentally-friendly policies

Ethical employment practices

Ethical business practices

43   BENEFITS

(a) **Identify TWO benefits to the community from the list below if an organisation introduces corporate social responsibility policies.**

A   Employee absence from work

B   Use of corporate resources to benefit the community

C   Employees using voluntary days of absence from work to support charitable activities.

D   Greater use of recycled materials

(b) **Identify TWO benefits to the environment from the list below if an organisation introduces corporate social responsibility policies.**

A   Employee absence from work

B   Greater use of renewable resources to reduce waste

C   Employees using voluntary days of absence from work to support charitable activities.

D   Greater use of recycled materials

44   CORPORATE SOCIAL RESPONSIBILITY

Which THREE of the following initiatives will minimise the environmental impact of an organisation's business activities?

• Ensuring company cars purchased have high CO2 emissions

• Offering free membership at a local gym

• Encouraging staff travel to work using public transport rather than using their cars

• Ensuring machines maximise energy consumption

• Installing energy saving production equipment

• Asking staff to leave their computers on overnight

• Installing motion sensor lights which turn off when rooms are empty

45 EMPLOYEE WELFARE

Which THREE of the following initiatives will improve the welfare of employees in an organisation?

- Introducing flexible working conditions for staff

- Ensuring all staff complete at least 8 hours overtime per week

- Offering all staff training and support to those who wish to gain further qualifications

- Opening the office at weekends to allow staff to work on Saturdays and Sundays

- Providing an onsite gym for all staff to use

- Offering bonuses to senior management staff only

LO4 UNDERSTAND THE IMPACT OF SETTING UP DIFFERENT TYPES OF BUSINESS ENTITY

46 THE ENTITY CONCEPT

Which of the following TWO statements describe the entity concept?

A   A person trading on their own with a view to making a profit

B   Transactions related to a business must be recorded separately from those of its owners and any other business.

C   Owners are not separate from the business

D   While recording transactions in a business we take into account only those events that affect that particular business

47 BUSINESS ENTITIES

Match the following entity to ONE description that best describes the entity:

Entity	Description
Sole Trader	An employee working on their own in the business office.
Partnership	A business owned by any number of shareholders.
Limited Company	A business owned and operated by one person
	An entity created for other purposes rather than profit
	A business owned and operated by two or more people

48 TAX IMPLICATIONS

Which one of the following is NOT applicable to a limited company?

A   Income tax and national insurance contributions on the profits

B   VAT on its purchases and sales

C   Corporation tax

D   Employer's national insurance contributions for any employees it has

49   OWNERSHIP V MANAGEMENT AND CONTROL

Identify whether each of the following statements is true or false.

A business does have to be owned and controlled by the same person   – True/False

A sole trader must work on their own   – True/False

Owners of a company are the shareholders and are managed by its directors.   – True/False

A partnership can employ managers to help run the business.   – True/False

50   LIMITED LIABILITY I

Indicate which of the following entities have limited liability or unlimited liability

Entity	Limited liability	Unlimited liability
A business owned and operated by one person		
A business managed by directors		
A business owned and operated by two or more people		

51   LIMITED LIABILITY II

Identify whether each of the following statements is true or false.

Limited liability means that a business does not have to pay its debts   – True/False

If a sole trader's business fails their personal assets are protected   – True/False

A partner is liable for the debts of the partnership if the business fails.   – True/False

Shareholders are limited in their liability if the company fails.   – True/False

Directors are personally liable if the company fails   – True/False

52   LEGAL ADMINISTRATION I

(a)   **Identify the FOUR records that a sole trader must maintain from the list below:**

- Customer List
- Sales and income
- Supplier List
- Expenses
- VAT paid and charged (if VAT registered)
- Personal assets
- PAYE deducted from employees' salaries

(b)   **Identify whether each of the following statements is true or false.**

Once the submission of tax return is complete these can be destroyed to save on storage costs   – True/False

These records must be kept for five years from the deadline for the submission of the tax return for the period to which they relate.   – True/False

53   LEGAL ADMINISTRATION II

Match the description of the legal documents of the company with an item from the picklist below:

Description	Documents
The statement confirms that no changes to key information have happened during the year. If changes have been made it states what they are.	
Must be approved and signed on behalf of the board of directors and a copy filed at Companies House.	
These are updated for changes in • members • directors and company secretary • charges • persons with significant control They are kept at the company's registered office and are available for public inspection.	
These must show: • details of all money received and spent • a record of assets and liabilities • statement of stocks at end of year. These need to be kept for six years.	

Picklist: Statutory registers, Profit and loss statement, Accounting records, Confirmation statement, Annual financial statements, Audit

54   BUSINESS FORMATION I

Match the statements about business formation to the correct entity

Statement	Sole Trader	Partnership	Limited company
There are no legal formalities.			
Must register for corporation tax with HMRC.			
They will need to register with HMRC for self-assessment of income tax.			
May have an agreement which sets out matters such as the share of profits			
There is a formal registration process with Companies House with a number of documents that need to be filed:			

55 BUSINESS FORMATION II

There are a number of important legal differences between companies and partnerships.

Which one of the following statements is not true?

A There are no formalities required to create a partnership

B A partnership does not need to register with HMRC to pay income tax

C Partners in a partnership are personally liable for the debts of the business

D A partnership must have a partnership agreement

56 PRE-INCORPORATION CONTRACTS I

Which of the following is incorrect with regards to a pre-incorporation contract?

A It is a contract by a person acting on behalf of an unformed company

B The company is bound by the contract.

C The company cannot enforce the contract against a third party

D The person who is acting on behalf of the company is personally liable

57 BUSINESS FORMATION III

Complete the following sentence using the pick list below

Once a company has been formed it is known as _____.

Picklist: Trading, Profit making, Incorporated, Off the shelf, Registered

58 COMPANIES HOUSE REGISTRATION

There is a formal registration process with Companies House with a number of documents that need to be filed.

Indicate which documents require submission to Companies House in order to incorporate a company.

Document	Required	Not Required
Memorandum of association		
Business plans		
Application for registration		
Statement of capital		
Statement of consent to act		
Statement of creditworthiness		
Statement of compliance		

59   PRE-INCORPORATION CONTRACTS II

An accountant entered into a pre-incorporation contract on behalf of C Ltd.

Which one of the following correctly identifies the person who may enforce the contract and against whom it is enforceable?

A   By and against the company only

B   By and against the accountant only

C   By the company and against the accountant

D   The contract is void as the company has not been incorporated

60   OFF THE SHELF COMPANY

Identify which TWO of the following are a disadvantage of buying an off the shelf company.

- Cheap and simple to buy

- May have unsettled liabilities

- Can trade immediately.

- No problem of pre-incorporation contracts.

- Can be more appealing to lenders

- Some documents will need to be submitted to Companies House which will need to be tailored to the company.

LO5 UNDERSTAND THE FINANCE FUNCTION WITHIN AN ORGANISATION

61   POLICIES AND PROCEDURES

Select THREE policies and procedures from the following list which are likely to apply to the finance function:

A   Data Protection

B   Health and Safety at Work

C   Curriculum policy

D   Authorised signatory procedure

E   Kitchen Hygiene policy

F   Administration of substances policy

62   DOCUMENTS

The accounts department of an organisation receives documents and information from other departments.

Match the department with the ONE document they would send to the accounts department:

Department		Document
Purchasing Department	(a)	Bank interest charged
	(b)	Copy of Purchase order
HR Department	(c)	Sales Commission
	(d)	New employee forms
Payroll Department	(e)	Statutory Sick pay forms
	(f)	Customer invoice

63   DEPARTMENTS

Match the following departments to ONE information type it would normally use:

Department	Information
Sales Dept.	Health and Safety guidelines.
Accounts Dept.	List of all new employees for the period.
Payroll Dept.	Bank statements.
	Commission payable to sales staff.
	Employee car registration numbers.

64   SERVICE PROVISION

Which TWO of the following services are staff in the finance function most likely to provide to staff in the sales department?

- Conducting job interviews
- Preparing sales brochures
- Budget report analysis
- Photocopier servicing
- Marketing new products
- Payment of sales commission

65   STAKEHOLDERS

Identify which TWO of the following stakeholders a trainee in the finance function is most likely to communicate with.

- People living in houses close to the organisation's Head Office
- The local MP
- H M Revenue & Customs
- The Head teacher of the local school
- Receivables
- An AAT examiner

66   REPORTING LINES

A business employs 2 Directors, 3 Managers and 6 Assistants.

Identify who each person should report to by selecting from the picklist. You may use an item more than once.

Person	Should report to the following
Sales and Purchase Ledger Assistant	
Administration Assistant	
3 Sales Assistants	
Payroll Assistant	
Accounting Department Manager	

Picklist: Managing director, Finance director, Sales manager, Accounts department manager, General manager

67   PERSON AND ROLE

Match which ONE person each role must report to:

Role	Reports to
Accounts assistant	Payroll manager
Sales ledger clerk	Finance director
Machine operator	HR manager
	Factory manager
	Accounting department manager

68 COMPLIANCE AND SOLVENCY

Select TWO actions that will ensure the legal compliance and two actions that will help the solvency of a business.

Action	Legal Compliance	Solvency
Ensure financial statements are filed on time.		
Improve credit control procedures.		
Maintain a petty cash book.		
Create and maintain a cash budget.		
Ensure the work place is a safe environment for staff and visitors.		

69 THE ACCOUNTING FUNCTION

The Finance function is an essential part of the business.

Select TWO actions for each of the columns. Actions should only be selected once:

Actions	Efficient running of the business	Solvency of the business	Legal Compliance
Monitor cash flow.			
Provide quotation to customer.			
Ensure Sales Tax is paid to HMRC on time.			
Regularly chase outstanding receivables.			
Ensure inventory is ordered when it falls to the minimum level.			
Ensure members of staff are first aid trained.			
Regular maintenance of machinery.			
Produce a staff rota for tea making.			

70 ISSUES

Some issues should be referred to a manager if they are unable to be resolved easily by an employee.

Which TWO of the following issues would you try to resolve yourself?

- The paper for the photocopier keeps running out without a new order being placed.

- You suspect a colleague is being harassed by another colleague.

- Your manager has requested you complete a task you do not have sufficient knowledge to complete.

- Somebody in the office continues to prop the fire door open.

71 PETTY CASH

Identify the most likely effect on the organisation if you were unable to complete the petty cash reconciliation on time.

- Your colleagues would be unable to complete their work on time.

- Fraudulent activity may have taken place and go undetected.

- Petty cash will be withdrawn, replaced with invoicing for small purchases.

72 CONFLICT

Some issues may lead to conflict in the workplace.

Indicate which issues can be resolved by you and which should be referred to your line manager.

Issue	Resolve myself	Refer to line manager
Your manager has asked you to complete a Statement of Financial position, however you do not have the accounting knowledge to do this.		
You suspect your colleague knows your computer password.		
You suspect an expenses form which has been passed to you has non-business expenses on it and the form has been submitted by a manager.		

73 OUTSOURCING

Sublime sauces Ltd is a small company that manufactures premium sauces and condiments. There are 30 employees of which 3 work in the finance function. Recently, the payroll clerk resigned and the managing director is considering outsourcing the payroll function to a payroll services company.

What factors should the managing director consider before making his/her decision?

74   COMMUNICATION

Good communication is the process of passing information and understanding from one person to another person (or group of people).

Match the following descriptions to the appropriate activity within the communication process.

Activity	Description
Encoding	The response to the message. It may be a simple acknowledgement of receipt and that the message is understood or a request for clarification or additional information.
Transmitting	The sender deciding what information needs to be communicated.
Decoding	The recipient receiving and understanding the message.
Feedback	Anything that undermines or prevents the successful transmission of a message.
Noise/interference	The means of communication used.

75   OVERDRAFT

The finance director at Flexiflo Ltd is concerned about the company's solvency over the next 12 months. He/she has asked the finance function to produce a cash forecast.

The following summary has been produced:

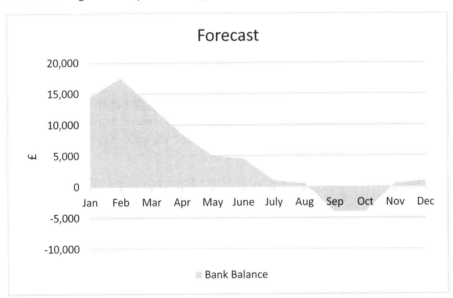

When should the Finance Director ensure that an overdraft facility is available and how much should he/she request from the bank?

LO6 PRODUCE WORK IN APPROPRIATE FORMATS AND COMMUNICATE EFFECTIVELY

76   MRS MAY

In your role as Financial Assistant you have recently received a purchase invoice (invoice number 3576) from Maybe Ltd relating to the purchase of 10 units of product ZXY. The invoice applied a cost per unit of £63, instead of the correct cost per unit of £36.

Draft a letter to Mrs May of Maybe Ltd to request a credit note to cancel that invoice and also to request a corrected invoice so that payment can be made, ensuring that you include all relevant information.

77   BILLY

Below is a response to a customer complaint.

Please highlight five words that are spelt incorrectly, or are inappropriate:

Dear Billy,

I was very cheesed to here that you did not receive your goods in proper working order. We have very strict internal procedures, which are designed to prevent faulty goods reaching our customers. Please be assured that we are investigating fully you're case and are striving to ensure that this does not happen again in the future.

By way of an apololy we will be refunding you in full and offering you a 20% discount off your next purchase.

Kind regards

John Anderson

Store manager

78   MR CADBURY

Review the draft correspondence below highlighting the spelling errors and inappropriate wording used.

Dear Mr Cadbury

I enclose a copy of the invoice which your requested during are telephone conversation this morning.

Please note this invoice is dated 31 June and therefor is overdue for payment.

I look forward to receiving your cheque in full settlement by return of post.

Yours faithfully

79   BOB

You are the manager of an accountancy firm (bob – bob@accountancyfirm.co.uk)

You want to discuss the exam performance of the AAT trainees with the training manager, Ally Mckoist (ally@accountancyfirm.co.uk) tomorrow afternoon. One student in particular (John Barnes) has performed poorly.

Draft an email to Ally.

From: bob@accountancyfirm.co.uk

To:

Subject:

80   K KIPLING

Draft an email which confirms an appointment with a client, Mr K Kipling (kk@cakes4tea.org.uk), to take place at his premises on Monday at 2.30 pm to discuss the business plan for the forthcoming year with Mrs Anna Howes.

From: AATstudent@Kaplan.co.uk
To:
Subject:

81   JOSHUA VALENTINE

The following is a partially completed email to inform Joshua Valentine (jvalentine@atoz.org.uk), Carmel Jenton (cjenton@atoz.org.uk) and Dane Wheeler (dwheeler@atoz.org.uk) of a conference on Thursday at 10am in the King's Hotel. The conference is being held to cover the issue of recycling within organisations.

Please complete as appropriate.

From: AATstudent@atoz.org.uk
To: _____   _____
Subject: _____
Hello All,
This conference is being held at _____ on _____ at _____am.
The conference will be held regarding the issue of recycling within organisations.
Please confirm your attendance.
Regards,
AAT Student

82 PURCHASE OF LAPTOPS

Your employer, K.P. Little has a surplus of cash in October 20X8 and it has decided to approve the purchase of 6 new laptops for the sales team.

The total cost approved for the laptops is £6,000.

Draft an email, dated 2 October 20X8, to Joe Wriggle (j.wriggle@kplittle.co.uk) the sales manager to make him aware of this news.

You need to ensure that Joe lets the sales team know that they will be provided with the new laptops.

Your name is Bernie Coalie and your email address is: (b.coalie@kplittle.co.uk).

To:
From:
Subject:
Date:

83 REPORT CONTENT

What information is usually contained within the areas of a report listed below?

	Introduction	Appendices
Information regarding what the report is based upon.		
Supporting calculations for figures contained within the body of the report.		

The following information is in respect of questions 84 to 90.

Murphy's Muffins provide cakes for weddings and corporate events. The company has grown significantly in recent years and has thirty employees working in administration, production, business development, marketing and accounts. Their customers include hotels and venues, events companies, corporate clients and couples soon to marry.

84 The Managing Director of Murphy's Muffins, Claire, is keen to promote the products and services she can offer to local businesses.

Which of the following would be the most appropriate way to communicate with potential business clients who Claire has not met previously? Tick the best option.

	✓
A memo	
A business report	
An e-mail	
A mobile phone text message	

85 Claire is keen to attend a local wedding exhibition to promote the cakes and novelty services her company, Murphy's Muffins, can offer to couples getting married. She has been asked to provide some text about the company for use in a brochure to be given to all attendees at the exhibition.

Which of the following should Claire include in the brochure? Tick the most appropriate option.

	✓
An outline of the company and what it does	
The full financial statements of the company	
A business report analysing other companies providing wedding services	
Her personal CV, including her education and past work experience	

86 The wedding exhibition has gone well and Claire needs to get in touch with the contacts she has made. A local businessman, Steven Crowfoot of Badger Events, is keen for Murphy's Muffins to attend a caravan exhibition in Birmingham he is co-ordinating and asks Claire to send him a proposal in writing.

How should Claire start the letter? Tick the best option from those provided.

	✓
Hi Steven	
Hello	
Dear Mr Crowfoot	
Dear Badger	

87 How should Claire end her letter to Steven Crowfoot of Badger Events regarding the caravan exhibition? Tick the best option from those provided.

	✓
Thanks for everything, Claire	
Best wishes, Claire	
Yours faithfully, Claire	
Yours sincerely, Claire	

88 At the wedding exhibition, Claire meets several couples who are soon to be married. She decides to send them all an e-mail the following week to remind them about Murphy's Muffins.

Which of the following would the most appropriate way for her to end her e-mail to the members of the public? Tick the most appropriate answer.

	✓
See you later, Claire	
Kind regards, Claire	
Yours faithfully, Claire	
Yours sincerely, Claire	

89 Having received communication from one of the couples looking to use her cake-making services for their wedding, Claire is asked to provide a quote for making 100 muffins for use throughout the day.

Which of the following would NOT be required as part of this quote?

A   Quantity of muffins required

B   Price per muffin

C   Payment terms

D   The actual cost of production of the muffins

90 As a result of an enquiry from the website, Murphy's Muffins has been asked to provide Christmas-themed muffins at a Winter Wonderland event in Bristol. Claire needs to inform all of her staff of the timings, location and agreed terms of their attendance at the event.

Which is the best form of business communication for Claire to inform her colleagues of the key facts?

A   A memo

B   A letter

C   A business report

D   Phone calls

LO7 UNDERSTAND THE IMPORTANCE OF INFORMATION TO BUSINESS OPERATIONS

91 INFORMATION

(a) Identify the FIVE key characteristics of useful information from the list below:

- understandable
- relevant and reliable
- legible
- consistent
- timely
- credible
- fit for purpose
- comparable

(b) Identify whether each of the following statements is TRUE or FALSE.

- Only information stated in monetary terms is useful to accountants
  – True/False

- Non-financial information is useful information to individuals who make decisions
  – True/False

92 NEW CUSTOMER

Cool Bearings Ltd is a manufacturer. They recently offered 90 days credit to a new customer. The balance remains unpaid and is currently 92 days old. Cool Bearings Ltd is considering whether to recognise this as a bad debt in the financial statements.

The finance director, Sarah, wants a decision made quickly so that the financial statements can be completed and issued soon.

However, the financial controller, Amit, argues that because the customer is new and only a little overdue, it would be better to wait a month in order to see whether the customer pays – he says 'it's better to be right, than quick'.

Identify which characteristics of useful information are being applied by Sarah and Amit.

	Characteristic
Sarah	
Amit	

Select from the list below:

- Comparable
- Consistent
- Understandable
- Relevant and reliable
- Timely

93 PEPPER & MINT

Pepper & Mint Ltd are an online clothes retailer. Customers have to set-up an account on the website before they can purchase from the company. The company has decided not to offer a 'guest' option where customers can purchase without setting up an account.

What are the advantages and disadvantages of this approach?

94 INVENTORY

The finance function have been tasked with ensuring that suppliers are only paid for goods actually received and accepted into inventory.

Which document will need to be received by the finance function so that they can confirm this?

Select from the list below:

- Purchase requisition form
- Purchase order form
- Supplier's despatch note
- Goods received note
- Purchase invoice
- Supplier statement

95 FIRE!

Flint Ltd maintains its accounting records on a computerised system. It recently suffered a fire caused by a faulty electrical circuit in its offices. As a result, it has lost all of the data in its finance function and has had to suspend trading.

What measures could Flint Ltd have taken to address the risk that it would be unable to recover data as a result of a fire?

96 PASSWORD

Francisco is the payables ledger clerk at Angeles Ltd where he has worked for 4 years. A password is needed in order for anyone to log on to a PC in the office.

Francisco's password grants him access to the general ledger, payroll, bank and cash ledger, receivables ledger and payables ledger.

His password is QWERTY which he has used since he joined the company – in fact he uses the same password for everything as it is easy to remember. He also keeps a post-it note in his top drawer that says 'Password QWERTY' so that his colleagues can log on to his PC if they need to when he is not in the office.

What are the data security weaknesses in the above scenario?

97 REVENUE

College Caterers Ltd supply fresh food to sixth form colleges across the county of Hampshire. As the food is fresh, it is supplied on the morning of each day. Sixth form colleges are closed at weekends. The company's accountant has expressed concern that the revenue of the company has increased significantly without an obvious explanation.

A report has been produced showing daily revenue which is summarised in the bar chart below:

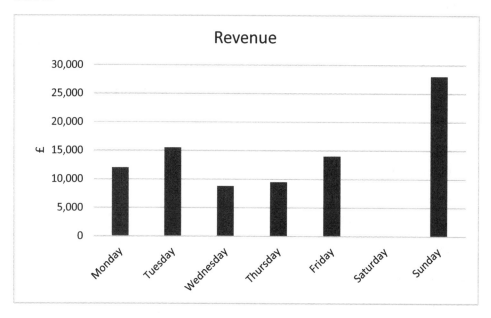

What is your key concern based on the above information?

98 RECEIPTS

Which of the following documents received by the finance function, can be used to match cash receipts from customers against the sales invoices to which they relate?

Select from the list below:

- Purchase order form
- Sales order form
- Despatch note
- Sales invoice
- Statement of account
- Remittance advice

99   BUDGETARY INFORMATION

The preparation of budgetary information is a responsibility of the finance function.

What purpose does budgetary information serve?

Select from the list below:

- To provide financial information to shareholders about the company's performance.

- To assist managers in decision making and control.

- To satisfy the requirements of the Companies Act.

- To provide information to the tax authorities.

100   CLOUD

The management of Cumulonimbus Ltd are considering investing a cloud accounting system.

Which of the following are advantages of such a system?

Select from the list below:

- It is unaffected by internet connectivity issues.

- Data can be accessed at any time, from any location, on a variety of devices.

- The accounting information is updated in real-time.

- The data is automatically backed-up by the cloud accounting service provider.

101   VIRUSES

How might a business protect itself from computer viruses?

102   DEPARTMENTS

Identify which department will make use of information supplied by the finance function.

Information supplied	Sales and distribution	Warehouse
Revenue broken down by customer		
Inventory holding period by inventory line		
Advertising expenditure by product range		

103   DEPARTMENTS (2)

Identify which department will make use of information supplied by the finance function.

Information supplied	Production	Payroll
National insurance rates		
Raw materials cost per unit		
Employee PAYE codes		

104   TECHNOLOGY

Identify whether the following statements are true or false.

Statement	True	False
Pre-set passwords set by the manufacturer must be changed to individually selected, unique passwords as soon as possible.		
The purpose of air-conditioning in the computer environment is solely for the comfort of those working in that environment.		

105   GOAL SETTING

Maria, the Finance Director at Sports Shorts Ltd wants to encourage staff in the warehouse to maintain inventory levels within a pre-determined range that minimises inventory holding costs whilst also ensuring that inventory is always on hand for customer orders.

She intends to set target quantities for each inventory line held.

Identify which TWO of the following sources of information would be most useful to Maria in setting these targets.

Select from the list below:

- Inventory movement records

- Sales records by inventory line

- Payroll information

- Customer contact details

Section 2

PRACTICE QUESTIONS

ITBK L01 UNDERSTAND HOW TO SET UP BOOKKEEPING SYSTEMS

106 LEO LTD

Leo Ltd codes all sales invoices with a customer code AND a general ledger code. A selection of the codes used is given below.

Customer	Customer account code
DEF Ltd	DEF14
Gamma Production	GAM27
MBG Co	MBG20
Harley Interiors	HAR18
Clarkson Wholesale	CLA16

Item	General ledger code
Standard bath	GL529
Standard washbasin	GL526
Luxury taps	GL530
Bathroom cabinet	GL521
Toilet	GL535
Standard light switch	GL528

<table>
<tr><td colspan="2" align="center">**Leo Ltd**</td></tr>
<tr><td colspan="2" align="center">**121 Apple Lane**</td></tr>
<tr><td colspan="2" align="center">**Cuddington, CU9 8EF**</td></tr>
<tr><td colspan="2" align="center">**VAT Registration No. 398 2774 01**</td></tr>
<tr><td>DEF Ltd</td><td></td></tr>
<tr><td>51 Neville Street,</td><td>18 Aug 20XX</td></tr>
<tr><td>Manchester, M1 4PJ</td><td></td></tr>
<tr><td>10 .... Luxury taps for washbasin @ £8.80 each</td><td>£88.00</td></tr>
<tr><td>VAT</td><td>£17.60</td></tr>
<tr><td>Total</td><td>£105.60</td></tr>
</table>

(a) Select which codes would be used to code this invoice.

General ledger code	Picklist: DEF14, GL529, GAM27, GL 526, GL530, GL521, GL535, CLA16
Customer account code	Picklist: GL530, GL526, DEF14, MBG20, HAR18, GL521, GL528, GAM27

(b) Why is it useful to use a customer code?

Picklist: To help when inventory (stock) taking

To help when completing a tax return

To help find the total amount due to a supplier

To help trace orders and amounts due from particular customers

107 ELLA'S PAINTS

Ella's Paint's codes all purchases invoices with a supplier code AND a general ledger code. A selection of the codes used is given below.

Supplier	Supplier account code
Peak Ltd	PEA27
Marker Production	MAR19
MEG & Co	MEG20
Farley Interiors	FAR12
Hammond Wholesale	HAM16

Item	General ledger code
White Paint	GL360
Standard Roller	GL395
Standard Brush	GL320
Yellow Paint	GL370
Roller tray	GL330

This is an invoice received from a supplier.

<table>
<tr><td colspan="2" align="center">**Meg & Co**</td></tr>
<tr><td colspan="2" align="center">**12 Barker Street**</td></tr>
<tr><td colspan="2" align="center">**Leeds L1 4NZ**</td></tr>
<tr><td colspan="2" align="center">**VAT Registration No. 402 2958 02**</td></tr>
<tr><td>Ella's Paints
19 Edmund St,
Newcastle, NE6 5DJ</td><td>18 Feb 20XX</td></tr>
<tr><td>20 .... standard rollers @ £2.30 each</td><td>£46.00</td></tr>
<tr><td>VAT</td><td>£9.20</td></tr>
<tr><td>Total</td><td>£55.20</td></tr>
</table>

(a) **Select which codes would be used to code this invoice.**

General ledger code	Picklist: PEA27, MAR19, GL360, MEG20, GL395, FAR12, GL330, HAM 16
Supplier account code	Picklist: PEA27, MAR19, GL360, MEG20, GL395, FAR12, GL330, HAM 16

(b) **Why is it useful to use a supplier code?**

Picklist: To help when inventory (stock) taking

To help when completing a tax return

To help trace orders and amounts due to particular suppliers

To help trace orders and amounts due from particular customers

108 ROBERTO & CO

Roberto & Co codes all purchase invoices with a supplier code AND a general ledger code. A selection of the codes used is given below.

Supplier	Supplier account code
Alex Ltd	ALE1
Toyworld	TOY10
Pudding and Co	PUD4
Springclean Ltd	SPR7
Spoonaway	SPO3

Item	General ledger code
Food	GL18
Toys	GL72
Stationery	GL45
Cleaning Equipment	GL78
Kitchenware	GL29

This is an invoice received from a supplier.

Alex Ltd	
Cherry Way, Haworth, BD22 9HQ	
VAT Registration No. 248 2764 00	
Roberto & Co	
Roberto House	
Ashton, AS2 8TN	1 Jan 20XX
10 .... teddy bears @ £4 each	£40.00
VAT	£8.00
Total	£48.00

(a) **Select which codes would be used to code this invoice.**

Supplier account code	Picklist: ALE1, TOY10, PUD4, SPR7, SPO3, GL18, GL72, GL45, GL78, GL29
General ledger code	Picklist: ALE1, TOY10, PUD4, SPR7, SPO3, GL18, GL72, GL45, GL78, GL29

(b) **Why is it necessary to use a general ledger code?**

Picklist: To help when filling in a VAT return

To help when bar coding an item of inventory

To help find the total amount owing to a supplier

To help calculate expense incurred in a GL account

109 ACCOUNTING EQUATION 1

Financial accounting is based upon the accounting equation.

(a) **Show whether the following statements are true or false.**

Item	True/False
Assets less capital is equal to liabilities	
Assets plus liabilities are equal to capital	
Capital plus liabilities are equal to assets	

(b) **Classify each of the following items as an asset or a liability.**

Item	Asset or liability?
Inventory	
Machinery	
5 year loan	

110 CLASSIFICATION

Classify each of the accounts below by adjoining a line between the account and correct classification.

Accounts

Payables (PLCA)

Inventory

Commission received

Classification

Asset

Income

Liability

111 ACCOUNTING EQUATION 2

Financial accounting is based upon the accounting equation.

(a) **Show whether the following statements are true or false.**

Item	True/False
Capital is equal to assets plus liabilities	
Assets less liabilities are equal to capital	
Liabilities are equal to capital plus assets	

(b) **Classify each of the following items as an asset or a liability.**

Item	Asset or liability?
VAT owed to tax authorities	
Amounts owing to payables	
Money in the bank	

112 CAPEX

It is important to understand the difference between capital expenditure, revenue expenditure, capital income and revenue income.

Select one option in each instance below to show whether the item will be capital income, revenue income, capital expenditure or revenue expenditure.

Item	Capital income	Revenue income	Capital expenditure	Revenue expenditure
Receipt from sale of motor vehicle				
Receipts from credit sales				
Purchase of machinery				
Payment of electricity bill				
Purchase of goods for resale				

113 REVEX

It is important to understand the difference between capital expenditure, revenue expenditure, capital income and revenue income.

Select one option in each instance below to show whether the item will be capital income, revenue income, capital expenditure or revenue expenditure.

Item	Capital income	Revenue income	Capital expenditure	Revenue expenditure
Receipt from sale of machinery				
Payment of telephone bill				
Purchase of building				
Receipts from cash sales				
Receipts from receivables				

114 EXPENDITURE TYPES

It is important to understand the difference between capital expenditure, revenue expenditure, capital income and revenue income.

Select one option in each instance below to show whether the item will be capital expenditure, revenue expenditure, capital income or revenue income.

Item	Capital expenditure	Revenue expenditure	Capital income	Revenue income
Purchase of a new computer system				
Receipts from customers				
Receipt from sale of fixtures and fittings				
Payments of salaries to staff				
Purchase of cleaning materials				
Receipt of bank interest				

115 ASSET OR LIABILITY

(a)   Classify each of the following items as an asset or a liability.

Item	Asset or liability?
Factory building	
Money due to suppliers	
Car used in the business	

ABC Co has paid an electricity bill by cheque.

(b)   Complete the sentence below by selecting the correct option to show how this transaction will affect the accounts of ABC Co.

The expense electricity will **increase/decrease**; the asset of bank will **increase/decrease**.

116 ACCOUNTING EQUATION 3

Show the accounting equation by inserting the appropriate figures using the information provided below:

Note: All figures should be shown as a positive balance.

Assets and liabilities	£
Land & buildings	120,000
Cars & machinery	20,960
Amounts due from credit customers	4,900
Bank	12,500
Amounts due to credit suppliers	13,870
Loan	15,000

Assets £	Liabilities £	Capital £

117 MULTIPLE CHOICE 1

(a)   State whether each of the following costs should be treated as capital expenditure or revenue expense.

		Capital expenditure or revenue expense
(i)	Work to install additional, high-specification, electrical power cabling and circuits so that additional plant and equipment can become operational	
(ii)	Replacement of some loose and damaged roof tiles following a recent storm	
(iii)	Repainting the factory administration office	
(iv)	Modifications to the factory entrance to enable a large item of plant and equipment to be installed	

(b)   Which of the following statements best defines a statement of financial position?

A   It is a summary of income and expenditure for an accounting period

B   It is a summary of cash receipts and payments made during an accounting period

C   It is a summary of assets, liabilities and equity at a specified date

D   It is a summary of assets and expenses at a specified date

(c)   The double-entry system of bookkeeping normally results in which of the following balances on the ledger accounts?

	Debit balances:	Credit balances:
A	Assets and revenues	Liabilities, capital and expenses
B	Revenues, capital and liabilities	Assets and expenses
C	Assets and expenses	Liabilities, capital and revenues
D	Assets, expenses and capital	Liabilities and revenues

118 MULTIPLE CHOICE 2

(a)   Which of the following statements best defines a statement of profit or loss?

A   It is a summary of assets and expenses at a specified date

B   It is a summary of cash receipts and payments made during an accounting period

C   It is a summary of assets, liabilities and equity at a specified date

D   It is a summary of income and expenditure for an accounting period

(b)   Which one of the following statements is correct?

A   Assets and liabilities normally have credit balances

B   Liabilities and revenues normally have debit balances

C   Assets and revenues normally have credit balances

D   Assets and expenses normally have debit balances

(c) **Which one of the following statements is not correct?**

A   A credit balance exists where the total of credit entries is more than the total of debit entries

B   A debit balance exists where the total of debit entries is less than the total of credit entries

C   A credit balance exists where the total of debit entries is less than the total of credit entries

D   A debit balance exists where the total of debit entries is more than the total of credit entries

119 LEO

(a) **Given below are a number of Leo's transactions. For each transaction, tick the relevant box to indicate whether it is a cash transaction or a credit transaction.**

TRANSACTION	CASH	CREDIT
(i) Receipt of goods worth £140.59 from a supplier together with an invoice for that amount.		
(ii) Payment of £278.50 by cheque for a purchase at the till.		
(iii) Receipt of a deposit of £15.00 for goods.		
(iv) Sending of an invoice for £135.00 to the payer of the deposit for the remaining value of the goods.		
(v) Sale of goods for £14.83, payment received by credit card.		

(b) **Given below are a number of typical transactions and balances that might be found in a business such as that run by Leo. Fill in the boxes to indicate whether the items are assets, liabilities, expenses or income.**

(i)   Goods stored in the warehouse awaiting resale

(ii)   Electricity bill paid

(iii) Sale of goods

(iv)   Amounts owing from a customer

(v)   Rent paid for the factory building

(vi)	Amounts due to the owner	
(vii)	Amounts owed to suppliers	
(viii)	Cash held in the till	
(ix)	Machinery purchased for use in the factory	
(x)	Rent received for subletting part of the factory premises	
(xi)	Cash held in the business bank account	

120 ACCOUNT CODES

This task is about manual and digital bookkeeping systems.

Accounts need to be created for a new customer and a new supplier. Account codes follow the format shown below:

A letter C to indicate a customer account, or a letter S to indicate a supplier account.

The first 4 digits of the customer or suppliers name.

A 3 digit sequential number representing the number of customer or supplier accounts.

(a)   **Enter the account codes for the new customer and new supplier.**

Date	Customer name	Customer account code
1 August	Worthington Ltd	CWORT092
4 August	Moss Plc	

Date	Supplier name	Supplier account code
2 August	Morley & Sons	SMORL076
5 August	Chapman Ltd	

(b)   **Identify whether the following statements regarding digital bookkeeping systems are true or false.**

Statement	True ✓	False ✓
The reconciliation between the individual payables ledger and the control account is completed automatically		
General ledger accounts need to be manually balanced off to extract a trial balance		

(c)   A sales invoice for a credit customer has been entered as a sales credit note incorrectly in the digital bookkeeping system. Identify TWO consequences of this error.

Consequence	✓
The total sales value will be understated	
The business may despatch goods that have not been sold	
The total amount owed to payables will be understated	
The business may be paid for goods that have not been sold	
The business may pay the incorrect amount to a supplier	
The business will receive more money from a customer than they are expecting per their customer report	

(d)   Identify which document or statement would be used for each of the purposes below.

Summarising the transactions for a period and classifying them into relevant categories of income and expenditure to show the overall profit or loss for the period	
Detailing all of the transactions with a credit customer during the period and advising a credit customer of the balance outstanding on their account	
To summarise the balances on each of the general ledger accounts in order to begin the preparation of the financial statements	
To correct an invoice that has been prepared incorrectly by overstating the value of goods supplied	

Options:

Petty cash voucher

Trial balance

Statement of profit or loss

Bank statement

Invoice

Supplier statement

Credit note

121 PRINCIPLES 1

This task is about the principles of double entry bookkeeping.

At the end of the accounting period, a business had the following assets and liabilities.

Assets and liabilities	£
Motor vehicles	10,180.00
Cash at bank	4,367.45
Inventory	2,100.00
Receivables	4,589.45
Payables	8,392.48
Bank overdraft	1,536.97

(a)   Complete the table below showing the accounting equation.

Assets £	Liabilities £	Capital £

The following business transactions have taken place:

Purchased a van for use in the business and agreed to pay the supplier at a later date.

Sold some goods to a customer for cash, making a profit on the sale.

(b)   Identify the dual effect of these transactions, by selecting the correct options for each transaction below.

Transaction 1	
Effect	✓
Increase assets	
Decrease assets	
Increase capital	
Increase liabilities	
Decrease liabilities	

Transaction 2	
Effect	✓
Increase liabilities	
Increase capital	
Decrease capital	
Increase assets	
Decrease liabilities	

A trial balance has been extracted from a business' bookkeeping system.

(c)   Identify which side of the trial balance the following account balances would appear.

Account balance	Debit ✓	Credit ✓
Opening inventory		
Payables		
Drawings		

122 DIGITAL BOOKKEEPING

This task is about manual and digital bookkeeping systems.

A business has started to sell a new type of product, and therefore additional general ledger codes need to be created in the digital bookkeeping system. All general ledger codes are 4 digits, and follow the format below:

- Asset codes start 0, followed by a 3 digit sequential code that represents the number of asset codes

- Liability codes start 1, followed by a 3 digit sequential code that represents the number of liability codes

- Income codes start 2, followed by a 3 digit sequential code that represents the number of income codes

- Expense codes start 3, followed by a 3 digit sequential code that represents the number of expense codes

(a) **Enter the account codes for each of the new general ledger codes below.**

Details	Ledger code	Details	Ledger code
Sales – dog food	2019	Insurance expense	3072
Sales – dog bedding		Courier expense	
Sales – dog toys		Advertising expense	

(b) **Identify the coding system used in the general ledger.**

Coding system	✓
Alphanumerical	
Alphabetical	
Numerical	

An invoice for the purchase of a motor vehicle for use within the business has been entered as motor expenses in the general ledger.

(c) **Identify TWO consequences of this error.**

Consequence	✓
Assets will be understated	
Sales will be understated	
Purchases will be understated	
Expenses will be overstated	

(d) **Identify whether the following statements about digital bookkeeping are true or false.**

Statement	True ✓	False ✓
It is not possible to post a duplicate transaction using a digital bookkeeping system		
Digital bookkeeping systems can automatically post recurring entries		
The trial balance will automatically balance using a digital bookkeeping system		

123 PRINCIPLES 2

This task is about the principles of double entry bookkeeping.

(a) **Classify the following items by choosing from the available options (you may use each option more than once).**

Item	
Motor vehicles	
Insurance costs	
Drawings	
Payables	

Options
Assets
Liabilities
Income
Expenses
Capital

The transactions shown below have taken place and been entered into the general ledger.

(b) **Identify the opposite effect of each transaction. You should ignore VAT.**

Transaction	Dual effect 1	Dual effect 2	
Owner invests £20,000 cash into the business bank account	Increases assets		
Purchases a laptop computer for use within the business, paying in cash	Increases assets		Options:
Makes a sale to a customer realising a profit on the sale. Customer agrees to pay at a later date	Increases capital		Increases assets Decreases assets Increases liabilities Decreases liabilities Increases capital Decreases capital
Owner withdraws £10,000 cash from the business to pay for a private holiday	Decreases assets		
A credit customer pays the amount owed	Increases assets		

At the end of the accounting period, a business has the following account balances:

Item	Balance £
Office equipment	Unknown
Receivables	4,593.90
Cash	1,342.80
Bank loan	6,780.00
Inventory	1,030.00
Capital	3,486.70

(c) **Use the accounting equation to calculate the office equipment balance.**

£	

124 PRINCIPLES 3

(a) It is important to understand the difference between capital expenditure, revenue expenditure, capital income and revenue income.

Select one option in each instance below to show whether the item will be capital expenditure, revenue expenditure, capital income or revenue income.

Item	Capital expenditure	Revenue expenditure	Capital income	Revenue income
Purchase of computer equipment				
Receipts from credit sales				
Receipt from sale of motor vehicle (non-current asset)				
Purchase of motor vehicle				
Purchase of stationery				
Payment of rent				

(b) **Show whether the following statements are true or false.**

Statement	True ✓	False ✓
Assets less liabilities are equal to capital		
The business and owner are treated as two separate entities		
A debit increases an item of income		

(c) **Classify each of the following items as an asset or a liability.**

Item	Option	Options
Computer equipment		Assets
Petty cash		Liabilities
Money owed to suppliers		

ITBK L02 PROCESS CUSTOMER TRANSACTIONS

125 ALESSANDRO LTD

On 1 August Alessandro Ltd delivered the following goods to a credit customer, Palermo Wholesale.

Alessandro Ltd
8 Alan Street
Glasgow, G1 7DJ

Delivery note No. 24369
01 Aug 20XX

Palermo Wholesale   **Customer account code:** AGG42
17 Zoo Lane
Dartford
DH8 4TJ

40 standard baths, product code SB05

The list price of the goods was £62.50 each plus VAT. Palermo Wholesale are to be given a 12% trade discount and a 5% discount if they pay within 5 working days.

(a)   Complete the invoice below.

Alessandro Ltd
8 Alan Street
Glasgow, G1 7DJ
VAT Registration No. 398 2774 01

Palermo Wholesale   **Customer account code:**
167 Front St
Stanley
DH8 4TJ   **Delivery note number:**
                                            Date: 1 Aug 20XX
Invoice No: 327

Quantity	Product code	Total list price £	Net amount after discount £	VAT £	Gross £

Alessandro Ltd offers each customer a discount of 5% if they pay within 30 days.

(b)   What is the name of this type of discount?

Picklist: Bulk discount, prompt payment discount, trade discount

---

126 HLB WHOLESALE

On 1 February Painting Supplies Ltd delivered the following goods to a credit customer, HLB Wholesale.

Painting Supplies Ltd
19 Edmund St
Newcastle, NE6 5DJ

Delivery note No. 46589

01 Feb 20XX

HLB Wholesale   **Customer account code:** HLB24

98 Back St

Consett

DH4 3PD

20 tins of white paint, product code SD19

The list price of the goods was £15 each plus VAT. HLB Wholesale are to be given a 10% trade discount and a 4% discount if they pay within 4 working days.

(a)   Complete the invoice below.

Painting Supplies Ltd
19 Edmund St
Newcastle, NE6 5DJ

VAT Registration No. 402 2958 02

HLB Wholesale   **Customer account code:**
98 Back St
Consett
DH4 3PD   **Delivery note number:**

Date: 1 Feb 20XX   **Invoice No:** 298

Quantity	Product code	Total list price £	Net amount after discount £	VAT £	Gross £

Painting Supplies Ltd offer a discount of 10% if their customers buy from them.

(b)   What is the name of this type of discount?

[   ]

Picklist: Bulk discount, prompt payment discount, trade discount

127 MASHED LTD

On 1 August Hickory House delivered the following goods to a credit customer, Mashed Ltd.

Hickory House
22 Nursery Road
Keighley, BD22 7BD

Delivery note No. 472
01 Aug 20XX

Mashed Ltd   **Customer account code:** MA87
42 Moorside Court
Ilkley
Leeds, LS29 4PR

20 flower pots, product code P10

The list price of the goods was £5 per flower pot plus VAT. Mashed Ltd is to be given a 10% trade discount and a 4% early payment discount.

(a)   **Complete the invoice below.**

Hickory House
22 Nursery Road
Keighley, BD22 7BD

VAT Registration No. 476 1397 02

Mashed Ltd   **Customer account code:**
42 Moorside Court
Ilkley   **Delivery note number:**
Leeds, LS29 4PR

Date: 1 Aug 20XX

Invoice No: 47

Quantity of pots	Product code	Total list price £	Net amount after discount £	VAT £	Gross £

Hickory House offers each customer a discount if they buy over a certain quantity of goods.

(b)   **What is the name of this type of discount?**

```

```

Picklist: Bulk discount, prompt payment discount, trade discount

128 ROCKY RICARDO

On 1 December Rocky Ricardo delivered the following goods to a credit customer, Alpha Group.

Rocky Ricardo
1 Rocky Way
Middleton, M42 5TU

Delivery note No. 2132
01 Dec 20XX

Alpha Group   **Customer account code:** ALP01
Alpha House
Warwick
WR11 5TB

200 cases of product A, product code A1.

The list price of the goods was £10 per case plus VAT. Alpha Group are to be given a 10% trade discount and a 2% prompt payment discount.

(a)   Complete the invoice below.

Rocky Ricardo

1 Rocky Way

Middleton, M42 5TU

VAT Registration No. 298 3827 04

Alpha Group   Customer account code:

Alpha House

Warwick   Delivery note number:

WR11 5TB

                                                Date: 1 Dec 20XX

Invoice No: 950

Quantity of cases	Product code	Total list price £	Net amount after discount £	VAT £	Gross £

(b)   What will be the amounts entered into the sales daybook after the invoice in (a) has been prepared?

Sales daybook

Date 20XX	Details	Invoice No:	Total £	VAT £	Net £
1 Dec	Alpha Group	950			

A cheque for £1,000 has now been received from Alpha Group which incorrectly states is full settlement of their account. Their account in the receivables ledger is shown below:

Alpha Group

Date 20XX	Details	Amount £	Date 20XX	Details	Amount £
1 Oct	Balance b/f	4,288	3 Oct	Bank	4,288
21 Nov	Invoice 123	1,500	25 Nov	Credit note 102	500
29 Nov	Invoice 189	2,000			

(c)   Which item has not been included in the payment?

┌─────────────────────────────────┐
│   │
└─────────────────────────────────┘

Select your account name from the following list: Balance b/f, Invoice 123, Invoice 189, Bank, Credit note 102

(d)   An invoice has been sent to Alpha Group for £500 plus VAT of £100. A prompt payment discount of 1% has been offered for payment within 5 days.

   (i)   What is the amount Alpha Group should pay if payment is made within 5 days?

   ┌─────────────────────────────────┐
   │ £   │
   └─────────────────────────────────┘

   (ii)   What is the amount Alpha Group should pay if payment is NOT made within 5 days?

   ┌─────────────────────────────────┐
   │ £   │
   └─────────────────────────────────┘

129   SDB

Sales invoices have been prepared and partially entered in the sales daybook, as shown below.

(a)   Complete the entries in the sales daybook by inserting the appropriate figures for each invoice.

(b)   Total the last five columns of the sales daybook.

Sales daybook

Date 20XX	Details	Invoice number	Total £	VAT £	Net £	Sales type 1 £	Sales type 2 £
31 Dec	Poonams	105	3,600				3,000
31 Dec	D. Taylor	106		1,280		6,400	
31 Dec	Smiths	107	3,840		3,200		3,200
	Totals						

130 MAHINDRA LTD

Sales invoices have been received and partially entered in the sales daybook of Mahindra Ltd, as shown below.

(a) Complete the entries in the sales daybook by inserting the appropriate figures for each invoice.

(b) Total the last five columns of the sales daybook.

Sales daybook

Date 20XX	Details	Invoice number	Total £	VAT £	Net £	Sales type 1 £	Sales type 2 £
31 Jan	Square Ltd	3567			1,000	1,000	
31 Jan	Oval & Co	3568		1,600			8,000
31 Jan	Diamond Ltd	3569	13,200				11,000
31 Jan	Triangle Ltd	3570		1,320		6,600	
	Totals						

131 PAR FOR THE COURSE GOLF SUPPLIES

Customer invoice number 2808 is being prepared based on the following customer quotation.

Par for the Course Golf Supplies Ltd

To: Erehwon Golf Club   Date: 13 August 20XX

Customer code: EREH094

Further to your enquiry, we are pleased to provide a quotation for the supply of:

300 units of product 107:

Pack of 12 golf balls @ £5.40 each (discounted to £5.00 each for purchases of 250 units or more)

150 units of product 119:   Golf umbrellas @ £7.90 each

Plus VAT at 20%

Payment terms: 30 days from end of month of invoice.

(a) Identify which type of discount was offered to the customer.

Discount type	✓
Prompt payment	
Trade	
Bulk	

(b) Calculate the amounts to include on the customer invoice.

	£
Net amount after discounts	
VAT @ 20%	
Total	

(c) Enter the invoice into the digital bookkeeping system by selecting the correct menu option, and making the necessary accounting entries.

Menu option	✓
Purchases daybook	
Purchase returns daybook	
Cash book	
Sales daybook	
Sales returns daybook	
Discounts allowed daybook	
Discounts received daybook	

Date	Customer code	Customer	General ledger code	Invoice number	Net £	VAT code
13 Aug		Erehwon Golf Club	Option 1			Option 2

Option 1	✓
1001 Sales – golf equipment	
1002 Sales – golf buggies	
4001 Purchases – golf equipment	
7001 Receivables	

Option 2	✓
V0 – 0%	
V5 – 5%	
V20 – 20%	

132 LINKEES TOY MAKERS LTD

Customer invoice number 2808 is being prepared based on the following customer quotation.

Linkees Toy Makers Ltd
To: Thomas' Toys   Date: 17 May 20XX
Customer code: THOM08
Further to your enquiry, we are pleased to provide a quotation for the supply of:
150 units of product B64: Board games (assorted) @ £4.50 each
Plus VAT at 20%
Payment terms: 30 days from end of month of invoice. 5% discount if payment received within 14 days from date of invoice.

(a) **Identify which type of discount has been offered to the customer.**

Discount type	✓
Prompt payment	
Trade	
Bulk	

(b) **Calculate the amounts to include on the customer invoice.**

	£
Net amount after discounts	
VAT @ 20%	
Total	

(c) **Enter the invoice into the digital bookkeeping system by selecting the correct menu option, and making the necessary entries.**

Menu option	✓
Purchases daybook	
Purchase returns daybook	
Cash book	
Sales daybook	
Sales returns daybook	
Discounts allowed daybook	
Discounts received daybook	

Date	Customer code	Customer	General ledger code	Invoice number	Net £	VAT code
17 May		Thomas' Toys	Option 1			Option 2

Option 1	✓
1001 Sales – toys	
1002 Sales – board games	
4001 Purchases – Inventory	
7001 Receivables	

Option 2	✓
V0 – 0%	
V5 – 5%	
V20 – 20%	
V1 – Exempt	

133   WILLIAM & SAMMY LTD

The account shown below is in the receivables ledger of Hickory House. A cheque for £668 has now been received from this customer.

William and Sammy Ltd

Date 20XX	Details	Amount £	Date 20XX	Details	Amount £
1 June	Balance b/f	4,250	2 June	Bank	4,250
23 June	Sales invoice 255	1,876	15 June	Sales returns credit note 98	1,208
30 June	Sales Invoice 286	2,459			

(a)   **Which item has not been included in the payment?**

[   ]

Picklist: Balance b/f, Sales invoice 255, Sales invoice 286, Bank, Sales returns credit note 98

An invoice is being prepared to be sent to William and Sammy Ltd for £3,890 plus VAT of £778. A prompt payment discount of 4% will be offered for payment within 10 days.

(b)   **What is the amount Hickory House should receive if payment is made within 10 days?**

£ [   ]

(c)   **What is the amount Hickory House should receive if payment is NOT made within 10 days?**

£ [   ]

134 DIAMONDS & RUBIES LTD

The following is a summary of transactions with Diamonds & Rubies Ltd, a new credit customer.

Invoice 3927, 5 August, £4,640
Credit note 96, 10 August, £980
Invoice 3964, 21 August, £1,560
Credit note 104, 28 August, £650
Cheque received, 30 August, £2,100

Complete the statement of account below.

Stavros

121 Baker St

Newcastle, NE1 7DJ

To: Diamonds & Rubies Ltd   **Date:** 31 Aug 20XX

Date 20XX	Details	Transaction amount £	Outstanding amount £
5 Aug	Invoice 3927		
10 Aug	Credit note 96		
21 Aug	Invoice 3964		
28 Aug	Credit note 104		
30 Aug	Cheque received		

135 MAX LTD

The following is a summary of transactions with Max Ltd, a new credit customer of Painting Supplies Ltd.

Invoice 4658, 5 Feb. £2,560
Invoice 3964, 11 Feb, £3,290
Credit note 125, 21 Feb, £230
Credit note 139, 23 Feb, £560
Cheque received, 27 Feb, £1,900

Complete the statement of account below.

<table>
<tr><td colspan="5" align="center">**Painting Supplies Ltd**
19 Edmund St
Newcastle, NE6 5DJ</td></tr>
<tr><td colspan="3">**To:** Max Ltd</td><td colspan="2">**Date:** 28 Feb 20XX</td></tr>
<tr><td>**Date**
20XX</td><td>**Details**</td><td>**Transaction amount**
£</td><td colspan="2">**Outstanding amount**
£</td></tr>
<tr><td>5 Feb</td><td>Invoice 4658</td><td></td><td colspan="2"></td></tr>
<tr><td>11 Feb</td><td>Invoice 3964</td><td></td><td colspan="2"></td></tr>
<tr><td>21 Feb</td><td>Credit note 125</td><td></td><td colspan="2"></td></tr>
<tr><td>23 Feb</td><td>Credit note 139</td><td></td><td colspan="2"></td></tr>
<tr><td>27 Feb</td><td>Cheque received</td><td></td><td colspan="2"></td></tr>
</table>

136 BETA BOARDS

The following is a summary of transactions with Ava Ltd, a new credit customer of Beta Boards

£350 re invoice 222 of 10 Aug
Cheque for £225 received 12 Aug
£744 re invoice 305 of 15 Aug
£339 re credit note 194 on 20 Aug
Cheque for £530 received 24 Aug

Complete the statement of account below.

<table>
<tr><td colspan="5" align="center">**Beta Boards**
3 Victoria Avenue
Troon
KA5 2BD</td></tr>
<tr><td colspan="3">**To:** Ava Ltd</td><td colspan="2">**Date:** 31 Aug 20XX</td></tr>
<tr><td>**Date**
20XX</td><td>**Details**</td><td>**Transaction amount**
£</td><td colspan="2">**Outstanding amount**
£</td></tr>
<tr><td>10 Aug</td><td>Invoice 222</td><td></td><td colspan="2"></td></tr>
<tr><td>12 Aug</td><td>Cheque</td><td></td><td colspan="2"></td></tr>
<tr><td>15 Aug</td><td>Invoice 305</td><td></td><td colspan="2"></td></tr>
<tr><td>20 Aug</td><td>Credit note 194</td><td></td><td colspan="2"></td></tr>
<tr><td>24 Aug</td><td>Cheque</td><td></td><td colspan="2"></td></tr>
</table>

137 BELLA PUMPKIN

The following is a summary of transactions up to 31 December 20XX for Bella Pumpkin, a new credit customer of Rocky Ricardo.

> £1,700 re invoice 1001 of 12 December
>
> £2,350 re invoice 1004 of 21 December
>
> £940 re credit note 101 of 21 December
>
> £470 re invoice 1010 of 27 December
>
> Cheque for £2,000 received 29 December

(a)   Enter the transactions into the receivables ledger of Bella Pumpkin.

(b)   Insert the balance carried down and the balance brought down together with date and details.

Bella Pumpkin

Date 20XX	Details	Amount £	Date 20XX	Details	Amount £

(c)   Complete the statement of account below to be sent to Bella Pumpkin

Rocky Ricardo

1 Rocky Way

Middleton, M42 5TU

To: Bella Pumpkin   **Date:** 31 Dec 20XX

Date 20XX	Details	Transaction amount £	Outstanding amount £

138 LAYLA LTD

Layla Ltd received two cheques from Heba & Co totalling £3,361.26, as detailed in the remittance advices below. The customer has been offered a prompt payment discount of 5% for payment within 10 days.

<table>
<tr><td colspan="2">Heba & Co

Remittance advice 3671

16 Aug 20XX</td><td colspan="2">Heba & Co

Remittance advice 3684

22 Aug 20XX</td></tr>
<tr><td>Invoice</td><td>£</td><td>Invoice</td><td>£</td></tr>
<tr><td>1028</td><td>473.87</td><td>1068</td><td>789.48</td></tr>
<tr><td>1046</td><td>1,006.62</td><td>1096</td><td>629.09</td></tr>
<tr><td>1059</td><td>462.20</td><td></td><td></td></tr>
<tr><td>Total</td><td>1,942.69</td><td>Total</td><td>1,418.57</td></tr>
</table>

Company policy is to match each transaction with the remittance advice number to query any under or overpayment.

(a)   **Allocate the amounts received by identifying the appropriate action in the customer report below. You may use each action more than once.**

Transaction type	Date	Details	Amount £	Action
Balance b/f	1 Aug 20XX		473.87	
Invoice 1046	4 Aug 20XX	Goods	1,059.60	
Invoice 1059	9 Aug 20XX	Services	462.20	
Invoice 1068	10 Aug 20XX	Goods	789.48	
Invoice 1096	14 Aug 20XX	Goods	662.20	

Action
Allocate full amount – 3671
Query underpayment
Allocate full amount – 3684
Query overpayment

Trinity Pet Products have a policy of offering customers a 5% prompt payment discount for payment within 10 days of the invoice date.

(b)   **Complete the table below by calculating the amount that Trinity Pet Products should receive, assuming both customers take advantage of the prompt payment discount offered.**

Customer name	Invoice number	Amount before discount £	Amount after prompt payment discount £
Oliver John & Co	387	8,345.60	
Excelsior Ltd	395	4,562.40	

Trinity Pet Products received a payment from another customer qualifying for a prompt payment discount. However, the prompt payment discount has been calculated incorrectly resulting in an underpayment.

(c)   **Complete the table below by calculating the amount that should have been paid and the amount that remains outstanding.**

Customer name	Prompt payment Discount %	Invoice amount £	Amount paid £	Amount that should have been paid £	Amount outstanding £
Galahad	5	7,529.40	7,093.52		

139   KLOPP & CO

Jurgen Ltd has received two cheques from Klopp & Co totalling £4,273.80, as detailed in the remittance advices below. The customer has been offered a prompt payment discount of 4% for payment within 7 days.

Klopp & Co Remittance advice 2976 17 Apr 20XX	
Invoice	£
Invoice 342	752.34
Invoice 354	475.61
Invoice 362	800.88
Invoice 371	235.68
Total	2,264.51

Klopp & Co Remittance advice 3018 24 Apr 20XX	
Invoice	£
Invoice 379	872.62
Invoice 383	649.23
Invoice 391	487.44
Total	2,009.29

Company policy is to match each transaction with the remittance advice number to query any under or overpayment.

(a) **Allocate the amounts received by identifying the appropriate action in the customer report below. You may use each action more than once.**

Transaction type	Date	Details	Amount £	Action
Balance b/f	1 Apr 20XX		752.34	
Invoice 354	2 Apr 20XX	Goods	475.61	
Invoice 362	9 Apr 20XX	Services	834.25	
Invoice 371	12 Apr 20XX	Services	245.50	
Invoice 379	13 Apr 20XX	Goods	1,051.34	
Credit note 46	14 Apr 20XX	Correction – 379	178.72	
Invoice 383	14 Apr 20XX	Goods	649.23	
Invoice 391	19 Apr 20XX	Goods	507.75	

Action
Allocate full amount – 2976
Query underpayment
Allocate full amount – 3018
Query overpayment

Henderson & Co has received a payment from a customer in full settlement of their outstanding balance. When Henderson & Co compare the amount received to the amount outstanding on their customer report, there appears to be an underpayment of £117.48.

(b) **Identify which TWO of the following would explain the reason for this underpayment.**

Reason	✓
The customer has taken a prompt payment discount of 6% that they were not entitled to, on an invoice of £1,958 before the discount.	
Henderson & Co have duplicated an invoice in their system for £96.90 plus 20% VAT.	
2 credit notes for £49.71 and £67.77 have been omitted by Henderson & Co.	
The customer has paid for £117.48 of goods that they never received.	

ITBK L03 PROCESS SUPPLIER TRANSACTIONS

140 NAN NURSING

A supply of chocolate puddings have been delivered to Nan Nursing by Pudding and Co. The purchase order sent from Nan Nursing, and the invoice from Pudding and Co, are shown below.

Nan Nursing

22 Nursery Road

Keighley, BD22 7BD

Purchase Order No. HH72

To: Pudding and Co

Date: 15 August 20XX

Please supply 50 chocolate puddings product code 742087

Purchase price: £20 per 10, plus VAT

Discount: less 10% trade discount, as agreed.

Pudding and Co

17 Pudding Lane, Bradford, BD19 7HX

VAT Registration No. 234 7654 00

Invoice No. 428

Nan Nursing

22 Nursery Road

Keighley, BD22 7BD

20 August 20XX

50 chocolate puddings product code 742087 @ £2 each	£50
Less Trade Discount	£10
Net	£40
VAT	£ 8
Total	£48

Terms: 30 days net

Check the invoice against the purchase order and answer the following questions.

(a) Has the correct purchase price of the chocolate puddings been charged?   Y / N

(b) Has the correct total discount been calculated?   Y / N

(c) What would be the VAT amount charged if the invoice was correct?   £_____

(d) What would be the total amount charged if the invoice was correct?   £_____

141 PIXIE PAPER

A supply of paper has been delivered to Alpha Ltd by Pixie Paper. The purchase order sent from Alpha Ltd, and the invoice from Pixie Paper, are shown below.

Alpha Ltd

121 Baker St

Newcastle, NE1 7DJ

Purchase Order No. PO1792

To: Pixie Paper

Date: 5 Aug 20XX

Please supply 50 boxes of A4 paper product code 16257

Purchase price: £10 per box, plus VAT

Discount: less 10% trade discount, as agreed.

Pixie Paper

24 Eden Terrace, Durham, DH9 7TE

VAT Registration No. 464 392 401

Invoice No. 1679

Alpha Ltd

121 Baker St

Newcastle, NE1 7DJ

9 Aug 20XX

50 boxes of A4 paper, product code 16257 @ £10 each	£500
VAT	£100
Total	£600

Terms: 30 days net

Check the invoice against the purchase order and answer the following questions.

(a)	Has the correct product been supplied by Pixie Paper?	Y / N
(b)	Has the correct net price been calculated?	Y / N
(c)	Has the total invoice price been calculated correctly?	Y / N
(d)	What would be the VAT amount charged if the invoice was correct?	£_____
(e)	What would be the total amount charged if the invoice was correct?	£_____

142   PAINTS R US

A supply of paint has been delivered to Painting Supplies Ltd by Paints R Us. The purchase order sent from Painting Supplies Ltd, and the invoice from Paints R Us, are shown below.

Painting Supplies Ltd

19 Edmund St

Newcastle, NE6 5DJ

Purchase Order No. PO6548

To: Paints R Us

Date: 5 Feb 20XX

Please supply 20 tins of blue paint, product code 23567

Purchase price: £8 per tin plus VAT

Discount: less 5% prompt payment discount, as agreed.

Paints R Us

19 Valley Gardens, Stanley, DH5 8JJ

VAT Registration No. 421 385 602

Invoice No. 2485

Painting Supplies Ltd

19 Edmund St

Newcastle, NE6 5DJ

10 Feb 20XX

20 tins of blue paint, product code 23567 @ £8 each	£160.00
VAT	£30.00
Total	£190.00

Terms: 30 days net

Check the invoice against the purchase order and answer the following questions.

(a)	Has the correct product been supplied?	Y / N
(b)	Has the correct net price been calculated?	Y / N
(c)	Has the total invoice price been calculated correctly?	Y / N
(d)	What would be the VAT amount charged if the invoice was correct?	£_____
(e)	What would be the total amount charged if the invoice was correct?	£_____

143 MT MOTORS

MT Motors purchased goods costing £500 from Z (before VAT at 20%). Z gave MT Motors a trade discount of 20%.

(a) **What was the net amount recognised as a purchase expense after the discount?**

    A   £480.00

    B   £400.00

    C   £600.00

    D   £333.33

(b) **What was the VAT on purchases after trade discount?**

    A   £100.00

    B   £80.00

    C   £20.00

    D   £94.00

(c) **Which one of the following statements best describes the purpose of a purchase order?**

    A   It is issued to a supplier to request supply of goods from them on terms specified within the order.

    B   It is issued to a customer to confirm the supply of goods to them on terms specified in the order.

    C   It is issued to a supplier as notification of payment.

    D   It confirms the price that will be charged by a supplier for goods supplied.

144 ECHO LTD

A supply of cardboard boxes has been delivered to Rocky Ricardo's by Echo Ltd. The purchase order sent from Rocky Ricardo's, and the invoice from Echo Ltd, are shown below.

Rocky Ricardo

1 Rocky Way

Middleton, M42 5TU

Purchase Order No. RR111

To: Echo Ltd

Date: 7 Dec 20XX

Please supply 1,000 widgets product code 243

Purchase price: £1 per widget, plus VAT

Discount: less 10% trade discount, as agreed

Echo Ltd

2 Walford Way, Essex, ES4 4XX

VAT Registration No. 533 8372 12

Invoice No. 123

Rocky Ricardo

1 Rocky Way

Middleton, M42 5TU

10 Dec 20XX

1,000 .... widgets product code 243 @ £1 each	£1,000.00
VAT	£200.00
Total	£1,200.00

Terms: 30 days net

(a) **Check the invoice against the purchase order and answer the following questions.**

Has the correct discount been applied? Y / N

How much should the trade discount amount be? £_____

What would be the VAT amount charged if the invoice was correct? £_____

The following invoice has been received from the credit supplier Messi Brothers.

Messi Brothers

Unit 3 Fothersway Business Park, Newcastle

VAT Registration No. 933 8982 02

Invoice No. 1365

Rocky Ricardo
1 Rocky Way
Middleton, M42 5TU

10 Dec 20XX

500 .... of product code 1872 @ £3.75 each	£1,875.00
VAT	£375.00
Total	£2,250.00

Terms: 30 days net

(b) **What will be the details and amounts entered into the daybook?**

Daybook:					
Date 20XX	Details	Invoice No:	Total £	VAT £	Net £
10 Dec		1365			

145 GORDON'S TRAIN REPAIRS

The supplier credit note below has been received.

Gordon's Train Repairs Ltd	
To: North Enozraw Railway	Date: 14 October 20XX
Credit note number: CN483	£
Correction of invoice no: 1859	476.50
VAT @ 20%	95.30
Total	571.80

(a) **Identify the daybook in which the credit note will be entered.**

Daybook	✓
Sales daybook	
Purchases daybook	
Cashbook	
Purchase returns daybook	
Sales returns daybook	
Discounts allowed daybook	

(b) **Complete the daybook by:**

- **Making FOUR entries to record the credit note**
- **Totalling the net, VAT and total columns.**

Date 20XX	Supplier	Credit note number	Net £	VAT £	Total £
17 May	Narrow Gauge Ltd	CN869	317.60	63.52	381.12
26 June	Island of Sodor plc	CN0289	84.00	16.80	100.80
8 Aug	Topham Hatt & Co	421	98.50	19.70	118.20
13 Sep	Flying Kipper Ltd	C980	206.00	41.20	247.20
14 Oct	Gordon's Train Repairs				
		Totals			

The invoice and goods received note below relate to an incorrect invoice received by North Enozraw Railway.

North Enozraw Railway

Goods received note GRN462

22 January 20XX

Goods received from Ulfstead Ltd:

10 iron girders

Received as ordered

Price per unit : £1,000 + VAT @ 20%

Ulfstead Ltd

To: North Enozraw Railway   Date: 22 Jan 20XX

Invoice no: 9362

Iron girders supplied	10 units @ 1,100	11,000
	VAT @ 20%	2,200
	Total	13,400

(c)   **Identify TWO discrepancies in the invoice received.**

Discrepancy	✓
Date of invoice	
Product type	
Quantity of product	
Unit price	
VAT rate	
Total	

146   NORMAN PRICE & CO

The supplier invoice below has been received.

Henry's Office Supplies	
To: Norman Price & Co	Date: 14 March 20XX
Invoice number: 7208	£
Supply and fit office desks × 2	584.00
VAT @ 20%	116.80
Total	700.80

(a)   **Identify the daybook in which the invoice will be entered.**

Daybook	✓
Sales daybook	
Purchases daybook	
Cashbook	
Purchase returns daybook	
Sales returns daybook	
Discounts allowed daybook	

(b)   **Complete the daybook by:**

- **Making FOUR entries to record the invoice**
- **Totalling the net, VAT and total columns.**

Date 20XX	Supplier	Invoice number	Net £	VAT £	Total £
8 Mar	Norris Ltd	3897	1,010.00	202.00	1,212.00
10 Mar	Sam Jones	0187	878.40	175.68	1,054.08
11 Mar	James & Sarah Ltd	402929	463.80	92.76	556.56
11 Mar	Trevor Dylis Ltd	73910	1,329.10	265.82	1,594.92
14 Mar	Henry's Office Supplies				
		Totals			

The following credit note and invoice relates to a prompt payment discount taken by Norman Price & Co.

George's Printer Repairs	
To: Norman Price & Co	Date: 28 March 20XX
Invoice number: 549	£
Printer repair work	675.00
VAT @ 20%	135.00
Total	810.00
Payment terms: 30 days from end of month of invoice. 2% discount if payment received within 14 days.	

George's Printer Repairs	
To: Norman Price & Co	Date: 4 Apr 20XX
Credit note number: CN45	£
To adjust invoice 548 for prompt payment discount	13.50
VAT @ 20%	2.60
Total	16.10

(c) **Identify TWO discrepancies between the invoice and the credit note.**

Discrepancy	✓
Prompt payment discount value	
VAT	
Invoice number	
Total	

147 FREDDIE LTD

Purchase invoices have been received and partially entered in the purchases daybook of Freddie Ltd, as shown below.

Novot & Co
5 Pheasant Way, Essex, ES9 8BN
VAT Registration No. 453 098 541
Invoice No. 2176
Freddie Ltd
9 Banbury Street
Sheffield
31 July 20XX
10 boxes of product code 14212 @ £400 each £4,000
VAT £800
Total £4,800
Payment terms 30 days

Purchases daybook

Date 20XX	Details	Invoice number	Total £	VAT £	Net £	Product 14211 £	Product 14212 £
31 July	Box Ltd	2177			800	800	
31 July	Shrew Ltd	2175		2,400		12,000	
31 July	Novot & Co	2176					
	Totals						

(a) **Complete the first two entries in the purchases daybook by inserting the appropriate figures for each invoice.**

(b) **Complete the final entry in the purchases daybook by inserting the appropriate figures from the invoice above and complete the daybook totals.**

148 ALPHA LTD

Shown below is a statement of account received from a credit supplier, and the supplier's account as shown in the payables ledger of Alpha Ltd.

<table>
<tr><td colspan="6" align="center">**ABG Ltd**</td></tr>
<tr><td colspan="6" align="center">**14 Hassle Street, Durham, DH9 7RQ**</td></tr>
<tr><td colspan="6">**To:** Alpha Ltd

121 Baker St

Newcastle, NE1 7DJ</td></tr>
<tr><td colspan="6" align="center">**STATEMENT OF ACCOUNT**</td></tr>
<tr>
<td>**Date 20XX**</td>
<td>**Invoice number**</td>
<td>**Details**</td>
<td>**Invoice amount £**</td>
<td>**Cheque amount £**</td>
<td>**Balance £**</td>
</tr>
<tr><td>1 May</td><td>468</td><td>Goods</td><td>7,600</td><td></td><td>7,600</td></tr>
<tr><td>1 June</td><td></td><td>Cheque</td><td></td><td>2,500</td><td>5,100</td></tr>
<tr><td>5 June</td><td>472</td><td>Goods</td><td>4,200</td><td></td><td>9,300</td></tr>
<tr><td>12 June</td><td>478</td><td>Goods</td><td>500</td><td></td><td>9,800</td></tr>
<tr><td>22 June</td><td>486</td><td>Goods</td><td>1,680</td><td></td><td>11,480</td></tr>
<tr><td>30 June</td><td></td><td>Cheque</td><td></td><td>2,000</td><td>9,480</td></tr>
</table>

<table>
<tr><td colspan="6" align="center">**ABG Ltd**</td></tr>
<tr>
<td>**Date 20XX**</td>
<td>**Details**</td>
<td>**Amount £**</td>
<td>**Date 20XX**</td>
<td>**Details**</td>
<td>**Amount £**</td>
</tr>
<tr><td>4 June</td><td>Bank</td><td>2,500</td><td>3 May</td><td>Purchases</td><td>7,600</td></tr>
<tr><td>28 June</td><td>Bank</td><td>2,000</td><td>8 June</td><td>Purchases</td><td>4,200</td></tr>
<tr><td>28 July</td><td>Purchase return</td><td>900</td><td>15 June</td><td>Purchases</td><td>500</td></tr>
</table>

(a) **Which item is missing from the statement of account from ABG Ltd?**

> [   ]

Picklist: Cheque for £2,500, invoice 468, Invoice 472, Purchase return £900, Invoice 486, Cheque for £2,000

(b) **Which item is missing from the supplier account in Alpha Ltd's payables ledger?**

> [   ]

Picklist: Invoice 468, Invoice 472, Invoice 478, Invoice 486, Purchase return £900, Cheque for £2,500

(c) **Once the omitted items have been recorded, what is the agreed balance outstanding between Alpha Ltd and ABG Ltd?**

> [   ]

149 **MAXIMUS LTD**

Alpha Ltd sends out cheques to suppliers on the last day of the month following the month of invoice. Below is an extract from the purchases (payables) ledger of Alpha Ltd.

Maximus Ltd

Date 20XX	Details	Amount £	Date 20XX	Details	Amount £
15 July	Purchases returns credit note 252	964	1 July	Balance b/f	5,980
21 July	Purchase return credit note 258	1,218	12 July	Purchases Invoice 864	6,386
31 July	Bank	5,980			

(a) Complete the remittance advice note below.

Alpha Ltd

121 Baker St

Newcastle, NE1 7DJ

REMITTANCE ADVICE

To: Maximus Ltd 20XX   **Date:** 31 Aug

Please find attached our cheque in payment of the following amounts.

Invoice number	Credit note number	Amount £
	Total amount paid	

(b) Are these two statements true or false?

A remittance note is for our records only   T / F

A remittance note is sent to a supplier to advise them of the amount being paid   T / F

150 HOLLY LTD

The account shown below is in the payables ledger of AD Wholesale. A cheque for £4,770 has now been paid to this supplier.

Holly Ltd

Date 20XX	Details	Amount £	Date 20XX	Details	Amount £
			5 Jan	Balance b/f	1,500
15 Jan	Purchase return 251	540	19 Jan	Purchase invoice 3658	2,360
31 Jan	Purchase return 286	360	27 Jan	Purchase invoice 2987	1,450

(a) **Which item has been not been included in the payment, causing it to be overstated?**

[ ]

Picklist: Balance b/f, Purchase invoice 3658, Bank, Purchase returns 286, Purchase invoice 2987

An invoice has been received from Rickman Repairs for £860 plus VAT of £172. A prompt payment discount of 10% will be offered for payment within 30 days.

(b) **What is the amount we should pay, if we meet the 30 days requirement?**

£ [ ]

(c) **How much VAT is payable if the payment is NOT made in 30 days?**

£ [ ]

(d) **What is the amount we should pay if payment is NOT made within 30 days?**

£ [ ]

151 EP MANUFACTURERS

Shown below is a statement of account received from a credit supplier, and the supplier's account as shown in the payables ledger of EP Manufacturers.

KLP Ltd

19 Mussell Street, Newcastle, NE4 8JH

To: EP Manufacturers
19 Edmund St
Newcastle, NE6 5DJ

STATEMENT OF ACCOUNT

Date 20XX	Invoice number	Details	Invoice amount £	Cheque amount £	Balance £
1 Jan	468	Goods	5,200		5,200
3 Jan	458	Goods	3,600		8,800
8 Jan		Cheque		1,400	7,400
19 Jan	478	Goods	800		8,200
21 Jan		Cheque		6,500	1,700
28 Jan	488	Goods	4,350		6,050

KLP Ltd

Date 20XX	Details	Amount £	Date 20XX	Details	Amount £
8 Jan	Bank	1,400	1 Jan	Purchases	5,200
21 Jan	Bank	6,500	3 Jan	Purchases	3,600
31 Jan	Bank	1,200	19 Jan	Purchases	800

(a)   **Which item is missing from the statement of account from KLP Ltd?**

Picklist: Cheque for £1,200, invoice 468, Invoice 478, Cheque for £6,500, Invoice 488, Cheque for £1,400

(b)   **Which item is missing from the supplier account in EP Manufacturers' payables ledger?**

Picklist: Invoice 468, Invoice 472, Invoice 478, Invoice 488, Purchase return £900, Cheque for £2,500

(c)   **Once the omitted items have been recorded, what is the agreed balance outstanding between EP Manufacturers and KLP Ltd?**

£

152 STANNY LTD

Ringo's Rings sends out cheques to suppliers on the last day of the month following the month of invoice. Below is an extract from the payables ledger of Ringo's Rings.

Stanny Ltd

Date 20XX	Details	Amount £	Date 20XX	Details	Amount £
13 Feb	Purchases returns credit note 198	650	1 Feb	Balance b/f	4,650
19 Feb	Purchase return credit note 154	1,250	10 Feb	Purchases Invoice 694	2,300
28 Feb	Bank	4,650	11 Feb	Purchase invoice 658	3,640

(a)   **Complete the remittance advice note below.**

<table>
<tr><td colspan="3" align="center">Ringo Rings</td></tr>
<tr><td colspan="3" align="center">37 Parker Lane</td></tr>
<tr><td colspan="3" align="center">Stoke SK1 0KE</td></tr>
<tr><td colspan="3" align="center">REMITTANCE ADVICE</td></tr>
<tr><td colspan="2">To: Stanny Ltd</td><td>Date: 31 Mar 20XX</td></tr>
<tr><td colspan="3">Please find attached our cheque in payment of the following amounts.</td></tr>
<tr><td align="center">Invoice number</td><td align="center">Credit note number</td><td align="center">Amount £</td></tr>
<tr><td></td><td></td><td></td></tr>
<tr><td></td><td></td><td></td></tr>
<tr><td></td><td></td><td></td></tr>
<tr><td></td><td></td><td></td></tr>
<tr><td></td><td></td><td></td></tr>
<tr><td colspan="2" align="center">Total amount paid</td><td></td></tr>
</table>

(b)   **Are these two statements true or false?**

A remittance note is for our and the supplier's records   T / F

A remittance note is sent by a supplier confirming amounts received from them   T / F

153 TOYWORLD

Shown below is a statement of account received from a credit supplier, and the supplier's account as shown in the payables ledger of Hickory House

Toyworld

18 Landview Road

Skipton

BD27 4TU

To: Hickory House

22 Nursery Road

Keighley, BD22 7BD

STATEMENT OF ACCOUNT

Date 20XX	Invoice number	Details	Invoice amount £	Cheque amount £	Balance £
1 Jan	207	Goods	2,500		2,500
8 April	310	Goods	900		3,400
9 June		Cheque		3,400	0
17 Aug	504	Goods	500		500
18 Aug	505	Goods	4,000		4,500

Toyworld

Date 20XX	Details	Amount £	Date 20XX	Details	Amount £
9 June	Bank	3,400	1 Jan	Purchases	2,500
25 June	Bank	500	8 April	Purchases	900
			17 Aug	Purchases	500

(a) **Which item is missing from the statement of account from Toyworld?**

Picklist: Invoice 207, Invoice 310, Invoice 504, Invoice 505, Cheque for £3,400, Cheque for £500

(b) **Which item is missing from the supplier account in Hickory Houses' payables ledger?**

Picklist: Invoice 207, Invoice 310, Invoice 504, Invoice 505, Cheque for £3,400, Cheque for £500

(c) **Assuming any differences between the statement of account from Toyworld and the supplier account in Hickory Houses' payables ledger are simply due to omission errors, what is the amount owing to Toyworld?**

£

154 HENRY HOUSE

Henry House sends out cheques to suppliers on the last day of the month following the month of invoice. Below is an extract from the payables ledger of Henry House.

Abbies Party Ltd

Date 20XX	Details	Amount £	Date 20XX	Details	Amount £
17 July	Purchases returns credit note 27	82	15 July	Purchases Invoice 242	220
			10 Aug	Purchases Invoice 764	44

(a) **Complete the remittance advice note below.**

Henry House

22 Nursery Road

Keighley, BD22 7BD

REMITTANCE ADVICE

To: Abbies Party

Date: 31 August 20XX

Please find attached our cheque in payment of the following amounts.

Invoice number	Credit note number	Amount £
	Total amount paid	

(b) **Which of the following statements is true?**

A   The remittance advice note will be sent to the Inventory Dept to advise them inventory has been paid for

B   The remittance advice note will be sent to the customer to advise them of the amount being paid

C   The remittance advice note will be sent to Henry House's bank to confirm payment is to be made

D   The remittance advice note will be sent to the supplier to advise them of the amount being paid

155   GREY GARAGES

Grey Garages makes payments to suppliers by BACS on the 25th of every month and includes all items that have been outstanding for more than 10 days.

Below is a pre-printed remittance advice slip taken from a statement of account received from a supplier, Mulberry Motors, showing all items outstanding.

Complete the remittance advice ready for the next payment to Mulberry Motors.

Remittance advice			
To: Mulberry Motors			
From: Grey Garages			
Payment method:		**Date of payment:**	

Items outstanding			**Tick if included in payment**
Date 20XX	**Details**	**Amount £**	
23-Jun	Invoice 213	740	
06-Jul	Credit note 14	120	
13-Jul	Invoice 216	620	
19-Jul	Invoice 257	870	
Total amount paid			£

156 ERRICO

The two invoices below were received on 5 June from credit suppliers who offer prompt payment discounts.

Invoices:

Giacomo

VAT registration 446 1552 01

Invoice number 1923

To: Errico   4 June 20XX

         £

4 product code 45 @ £14.50 each   58.00

VAT @ 20%   11.60

       ————

Total   69.60

Terms: 3% prompt payment discount if payment is received within 7 days of the invoice date.

Gaetani

VAT registration 446 4742 01

Invoice number 4578

To: Errico   4 June 20XX

         £

3 product code 42a @ £11.50 each   34.50

VAT @ 20%   6.90

       ————

Total   41.40

Terms: 5% prompt payment discount if payment is received within 5 days of the invoice date.

Calculate the amount to be paid to each supplier if the prompt payment discount is taken and show the date by which the supplier should receive the payment.

Supplier	£	Date by which the payment should be received by the supplier
Giacomo		
Gaetani		

157 LEWIN & CO

The two invoices below were received on 20 October from credit suppliers of Lewin & Co who offer prompt payment discounts.

Invoices:

Bridge Brothers	
VAT registration 446 4752 01	
Invoice number 193	
To: Lewin & Co 19 October 20XX	
	£
5 product code 895 @ £18.75 each	93.75
VAT @ 20%	18.75
	————
Total	112.50
Terms: 2% prompt payment discount if payment is received within 4 days of the invoice date.	

Mitchells	
VAT registration 446 4742 01	
Invoice number 578	
To: Lewin & Co 19 October 20XX	
	£
9 product code 756 @ £13.25 each	119.25
VAT @ 20%	23.85
	————
Total	143.10
Terms: 10% prompt payment discount if payment is received within 5 days of the invoice date.	

(a)   **Calculate the amount to be paid to each supplier if the prompt payment discount is taken and show the date by which the supplier should receive the payment.**

Supplier	£	Date by which the payment should be received by the supplier
Bridge Brothers		
Mitchells		

It is the policy of Lewin & Co to check each supplier statement as they arrive to ensure that they agree to the individual accounts within the payables ledger. Provided below is the statement of account from Xcess Stock and their account in the payables ledger.

Lewin & Co's policy is to only pay for items from the supplier statement which appear in their account in the payables ledger.

(b) Place a tick next to the 3 items in the supplier statement which will not be included within the payment.

Date 20XX	Details	Amount £	Date 20XX	Details	Amount £
21 Dec	Credit note 101	940	12 Dec	Invoice 1001	1,700
			21 Dec	Invoice 1004	2,350
31 Dec	Balance c/d	3,580	27 Dec	Invoice 1010	470
		4,520			4,520
			20XY 1 Jan	Balance b/d	3,580

Xcess Stock **Unit 7 Windy Industrial Estate** **Irvine, KA6 8HU** **To:** Lewin & Co **Date:** 31 Dec 20XX			**Not to be paid** ✓
Date 20XX	Details	Transaction amount £	
12 Dec	Invoice 1001	1,700	
13 Dec	Invoice 1003	1,500	
21 Dec	Invoice 1004	2,350	
21 Dec	Credit note 101	940	
22 Dec	Invoice 1005	450	
27 Dec	Invoice 1010	470	
28 Dec	Credit note 102	50	

(c) What will be the amount paid to Xcess Stock by Lewin & Co?

£

(d) One of the accounts within the payables ledger of Lewin & Co is for the credit supplier Minto Madness. A credit note for a prompt payment discount of £20 plus VAT has been received from Minto Madness. Before processing the credit note, the balance on the account of Minto Madness is £1,540.

What is the amount remaining on the account taking into consideration the credit note?

£

158 ASHBOURNE LTD

It is company policy at Ashbourne Ltd to only take advantage of prompt payment discount if the discount percentage is at least 5%. Below is a report from the digital bookkeeping system dated today, 13 January.

Supplier account code	Supplier name	Payment terms
K17	Kennack & Co	30 days
B07	Butterworth & Sons	30 days (4% discount for payments within 10 days)
J04	Jermyn Ltd	30 days (5% discount for payments within 7 days)

(a) **Identify the amount to be paid and the date by which the supplier should receive payment, for each of the invoices below:**

Supplier name	Invoice amount £	Invoice date 20XX	Amount to be paid £	Date by which supplier should receive payment
Kennack & Co	756.90	9 Jan		
Butterworth & Sons	1,317.83	11 Jan		
Jermyn Ltd	847.60	10 Jan		

Below is a statement of account from a supplier, as well as a supplier report from the digital bookkeeping system.

Farfield Ltd Statement of Account		
To: Ashbourne Ltd		30 June 20XX
Date 20XX	Transactions	£
1 June	Opening balance	639
4 June	Invoice 287	1,204
8 June	Invoice 294	897
11 June	Invoice 304	3,453
12 June	Invoice 307	257
18 June	Credit note 045	564
26 June	Invoice 342	1,865

Supplier report		
Farfield Ltd	Supplier code F009	
Date 20XX	Details	£
1 June	Opening balance	639
4 June	Invoice 287	1,204
8 June	Invoice 294	897
11 June	Invoice 304	3,453
12 June	Invoice 307	257
12 June	Invoice 307	257
18 June	Credit note 045	564
26 June	Invoice 342	1,865
30 June	CHQ 3672	5,296

(b) **Identify which THREE transactions shown on the supplier statement of account have already been paid.**

Transactions	✓
Opening balance	
Invoice 287	
Invoice 294	
Invoice 304	
Invoice 307	
Invoice 307	
Credit note 045	
Invoice 342	

(c) **Identify the type of error shown on the supplier report on the 12 June.**

Type of error	✓
Underpayment	
Overpayment	
Missing transactions	
Duplicate transaction	
Timing difference	

KAPLAN PUBLISHING

159 FARFIELD LTD

It is company policy at Farfield Ltd to always take advantage of prompt payment discount offered. Below is a report from the digital bookkeeping system dated today, 28 August.

Supplier account code	Supplier name	Payment terms
A09	Archer Joinery	Net monthly
S06	Sankey Electrical	2.5% discount for payments within 14 days
P05	Pannal Construction	3% discount for payments within 10 days

(a) **Identify the amount to be paid and the date by which the supplier should receive payment, for each of the invoices below:**

Supplier name	Invoice amount £	Invoice date 20XX	Amount to be paid £	Date by which supplier should receive payment
Archer Joinery	1,340.00	25 Aug		
Sankey Electrical	4,372.80	26 Aug		
Pannal Construction	3,720.00	26 Aug		

Below is a statement of account from a supplier, as well as a supplier report from the digital bookkeeping system.

Kelham Builders Statement of Account			Supplier report		
To: Farfield Ltd		31 Oct 20XX	Kelham Builders	Supplier code K06	
Date 20XX	Transactions	£	Date 20XX	Details	£
1 Oct	Opening balance	2,056	1 Oct	Opening balance	1,160
2 Oct	CHQ 0786	896	7 Oct	Invoice 308	945
7 Oct	Invoice 308	945	10 Oct	Invoice 314	1,342
10 Oct	Invoice 314	1,342	14 Oct	Credit note 048	897
14 Oct	Credit note 048	897	22 Oct	Invoice 326	2,085
22 Oct	Invoice 326	2,085	26 Oct	Invoice 338	451
26 Oct	Invoice 338	451	29 Oct	CHQ 0831	1,605
30 Oct	Invoice 343	846	30 Oct	Invoice 343	846

(b)   **Identify which THREE transactions shown on the supplier statement of account have already been paid.**

Transactions	✓
Opening balance	
Invoice 308	
Invoice 314	
Credit note 048	
Invoice 326	
Invoice 338	
Invoice 343	

(c)   **Identify the reason for the discrepancy between the opening balance on the supplier statement and the supplier report.**

Type of error	✓
Underpayment	
Timing difference	
Overpayment	
Missing transactions	
Duplicate transaction	

Section 3

PRACTICE QUESTIONS

POBC L01 USE CONTROL ACCOUNTS

160 MONSTER MUNCHIES

This is a summary of transactions with customers of Monster Munchies during the month of June.

(a) **Show whether each entry will be a debit or credit in the Receivables ledger control account in the General ledger.**

Details	Amount £	Debit ✓	Credit ✓
Balance of receivables at 1 June	48,000		
Goods sold on credit	12,415		
Receipts from credit customers	22,513		
Discount allowed	465		
Sales returns from credit customers	320		

(b) **What will be the balance brought down on 1 July on the above account?**

	✓
Dr £37,117	
Cr £37,117	
Dr £83,713	
Cr £83,713	
Dr £58,883	
Cr £58,883	

The following debit balances were in the subsidiary receivables ledger on 1 July.

	£
XXX Ltd	21,300
Brittle Homes Ltd	5,376
Colin and Campbell	333
Bashford Incorporated	1,733
Mainstreet Homes	3,426
Shamrock Interiors	4,629

(c) **Reconcile the balances shown above with the receivables ledger control account balance you have calculated in part (a).**

	£
Receivables ledger control account balance as at 30 June	
Total of subsidiary receivables ledger accounts as at 30 June	
Difference	

(d) **Which TWO of the following reasons could be explanations of why the total on a receivables ledger control account may be higher than the total of balances on a receivables ledger?**

	✓
Sales returns may have been omitted from the subsidiary ledger.	
Discounts allowed may have been omitted from the subsidiary ledger.	
Sales returns may have been entered in the subsidiary ledger twice.	
Discounts allowed may have been entered in the subsidiary ledger twice.	

It is important to reconcile the receivables ledger control account on a regular basis.

(e) **Which of the following statements is true?**

	✓
Reconciliation of the receivables ledger control account assures managers that the amount showing as owed to suppliers is correct.	
Reconciliation of the receivables ledger control account assures managers that the amount showing as outstanding from customers is correct.	
Reconciliation of the receivables ledger control account will show if a purchase invoice has been omitted from the payables ledger.	
Reconciliation of the receivables ledger control account will show if a purchase invoice has been omitted from the receivables ledger.	

161   JACK'S BOX

This is a summary of transactions with customers of Jack's Box during the month of April.

(a)   **Show whether each entry will be a debit or a credit in the Receivables ledger control account in the General ledger.**

Details	Amount £	Debit ✓	Credit ✓
Balance of receivables at 1 April	60,589		
Goods sold on credit	26,869		
Payments received from credit customers	29,411		
Discount allowed	598		
Goods returned from credit customers	1,223		

(b)   **What will be the balance brought down on 1 May on the above account?**

	✓
Dr £55,030	
Cr £55,030	
Dr £56,226	
Cr £56,226	
Dr £52,584	
Cr £52,584	

The following debit balances were in the subsidiary receivables ledger on 1 May.

	£
Olsen & Lane	19,455
Frith Ltd	625
Hodgetts & Co	412
Geevor plc	17,623
Trevaskis Farm Ltd	16,888

(c)   **Reconcile the balances shown above with the receivables ledger control account balance you have calculated in part (b).**

	£
Receivables ledger control account balances as at 30 April	
Total of subsidiary receivables ledger accounts as at 30 April	
Difference	

(d) **What may have caused the difference of £1,223 you calculated in part (c)?**

	✓
Sales returns may have been omitted from the subsidiary ledger	
Discounts allowed may have been omitted from the subsidiary ledger	
Sales returns have been entered into the subsidiary ledger twice	
Discounts allowed have been entered into receivables ledger control account twice	

It is important to reconcile the receivables ledger control account on a regular basis.

(e) **Which of the following statements is true?**

	✓
Reconciliation of the receivables ledger control account will show if a purchase invoice has been omitted from the payables ledger.	
Reconciliation of the receivables ledger control account will show if a sales invoice has been omitted from the payables ledger.	
Reconciliation of the receivables ledger control account assures managers that the amount showing due to suppliers is correct.	
Reconciliation of the receivables ledger control account assures managers that the amount showing due from customers is correct.	

162 CILLA'S SINKS

This is a summary of transactions with suppliers of Cilla's Sinks during the month of June.

(a) **Show whether each entry will be a debit or credit in the Payables Ledger control account in the General Ledger.**

Details	Amount £	Debit ✓	Credit ✓
Balance of payables at 1 June	52,150		
Goods bought on credit	19,215		
Payments made to credit suppliers	19,073		
Discount received	284		
Goods returned to credit suppliers	1,023		

(b) **What will be the balance brought down on 1 July on the above account?**

	✓
Dr £51,553	
Cr £51,553	
Dr £50,985	
Cr £50,985	
Dr £50,701	
Cr £50,701	

The following credit balances were in the subsidiary payables ledger on 1 July.

	£
BWF Ltd	19,563
All Parts Ltd	10,207
Hove Albion	4,501
Barton Groves	6,713
Cambridge Irons	5,913
Outside Arenas	5,111

(c) **Reconcile the balances shown above with the payables ledger control account balance you have calculated in part (a).**

	£
Payables ledger control account balance as at 30 June	
Total of subsidiary payables ledger accounts as at 30 June	
Difference	

It is important to reconcile the payables ledger control account on a regular basis.

(d) **What may have caused the difference calculated in part (c)?**

	✓
Goods returned may have been omitted from the subsidiary ledger.	
Discounts received may have been omitted from the subsidiary ledger.	
Goods returned may have been entered in the subsidiary ledger twice.	
Discounts received may have been entered into the subsidiary ledger twice.	

(e) **Which of the following statements is true?**

	✓
Reconciliation of the payables ledger control account will help to identify any supplier invoices that have been omitted in error.	
Reconciliation of the payables ledger control account will show if a sales invoice has been omitted from the payables ledger.	
Reconciliation of the payables ledger control account will show if a sales invoice has been omitted from the receivables ledger.	
Reconciliation of the payables ledger control account will help to identify any discounts allowed that have been omitted in error.	

163 VIK'S TRICKS

This is a summary of transactions with customers of Vik's Tricks during the month of June.

(a) **Show whether each entry will be a debit or credit in the Receivables ledger control account in the General ledger.**

Details	Amount £	Debit ✓	Credit ✓
Balance of receivables at 1 June	58,120		
Goods sold on credit	20,013		
Receipts from credit customers	22,327		
Discount allowed	501		
Sales returns from credit customers	970		

(b) **What will be the balance brought down on 1 July on the above account?**

	✓
Dr £58,963	
Cr £58,963	
Dr £57,277	
Cr £57,277	
Dr £54,335	
Cr £54,335	

The following debit balances were in the subsidiary receivables ledger on 1 July.

	£
Woffel Homes	21,026
Perfect Rooms Ltd	14,709
Brighton Dwellings Ltd	7,864
Grosvenor Homes	3,198
Oxford Designs	3,011
Indoor Delights	5,497

(c) **Reconcile the balances shown above with the receivables ledger control account balance you have calculated in part (a).**

	£
Receivables ledger control account balance as at 30 June	
Total of subsidiary receivables ledger accounts as at 30 June	
Difference	

(d) **Which TWO of the following reasons could be explanations of why the total on a receivables ledger control account may be LOWER than the total of balances on a receivables ledger?**

	✓
Discounts allowed may have been entered in the subsidiary ledger twice.	
Discounts allowed may have been omitted from the subsidiary ledger.	
Sales returns may have been entered in the subsidiary ledger twice.	
Sales returns may have been omitted from the subsidiary ledger.	

It is important to reconcile the receivables ledger control account on a regular basis.

(e)   Which of the following statements is true?

✓

Reconciliation of the receivables ledger control account will help to identify any customer invoices that have been omitted in error.	
Reconciliation of the receivables ledger control account will show if a purchase invoice has been omitted from the receivables ledger.	
Reconciliation of the receivables ledger control account will show if a purchase invoice has been omitted from the payables ledger.	
Reconciliation of the receivables ledger control account will help to identify any discounts received that have been omitted in error.	

164 ZHANG

When Zhang came to reconcile his RLCA with his list of balances on the receivables ledger, he found that they did not match. The RLCA had a balance of £65,830 and the list of balances totalled £65,090. Upon further investigation, he discovered that the following errors had been made:

1   The sales day book had been incorrectly totalled and had been overcast by £1,200.

2   A contra of £800 had been made in the RLCA, but had not been recorded in the receivables ledger.

3   A credit note of £130 had been posted twice in the receivables ledger.

4   A discount given of £210 had only been recorded in the receivables ledger.

(a)   Update the RLCA and list of balances to make sure that the two agree.

RLCA

Details	Amount £	Details	Amount £
Balance b/d	65,830		
		Balance c/d	
Balance b/d			

List of balances:

	£
Total	65,090
Revised total	

(b) Show whether the following statements are true or false:

	True ✓	False ✓
An aged trade receivables analysis is used when chasing customers for outstanding payments.		
An aged trade receivables analysis is sent to credit customers when payments are being requested.		

165 HANDYSIDE

When Handyside came to reconcile his PLCA with his list of balances on the payables ledger, he found that they did not match. The PLCA had a balance of £25,360 and the list of balances totalled £26,000. Upon further investigation, he discovered that the following errors had been made:

1   In the payables ledger, a purchase of £2,400 (including VAT at 20%) had been entered at the net amount.

2   Returns of £350 had not been included in the payables ledger.

3   An invoice for £600 plus VAT had not been posted in the PLCA yet.

4   Returns of £120 were missing from the PLCA.

5   An invoice for £340 had been entered into the payables ledger as £430.

(a) Update the PLCA and list of balances to make sure that the two agree.

PLCA

Details	Amount £	Details	Amount £
		Balance b/d	25,360
Balance c/d			
		Balance b/d	

List of balances:

	£
Total	26,000
Revised total	

(b)   Show whether the following statements are true or false:

	True ✓	False ✓
The payables ledger control account enables a business to see how much is owed to individual suppliers		
The payables ledger control account total should reconcile to the total of the list of supplier balances in the payables ledger		

166   RING TELEPHONE

The following is an extract from Ring Telephone's books of prime entry.

Totals for quarter

Sales day-book		**Purchases day-book**	
Net:	£153,000	Net:	£81,000
VAT:	£30,600	VAT:	£16,200
Gross:	£183,600	Gross:	£97,200
Sales returns day-book		**Purchases returns day-book**	
Net:	£1,800	Net:	£5,800
VAT:	£360	VAT:	£1,160
Gross:	£2,160	Gross:	£6,960
Cash book			
Net cash sales:	£240		
VAT:	£48		
Gross cash sales:	£288		

(a)   What will be the entries in the VAT control account to record the VAT transactions in the quarter?

VAT control

Details	Amount £	Details	Amount £

Picklist: Cash sales, Purchases, Purchases returns, Sales, Sales returns, VAT.

The VAT return has been completed and shows an amount owing from HMRC of £15,248.

(b)   **Is the VAT return correct?**   Yes/No

(c)   At the end of the next period, the VAT control account has debit entries amounting to £93,800 and credit entries amounting to £54,400.

The following transactions have not yet been recorded in the VAT control account:

VAT of £400 on purchase of equipment

VAT of £900 on cash sales

What will be the balance brought down on the VAT account after the transactions above have been recorded? Also identify whether the balance will be a debit or a credit.

	£	Debit	Credit
Balance brought down			

167   JO'S JOINERS

The following is an extract from Jo's Joiners books of prime entry.

Totals for quarter			
Sales day book		**Purchases day book**	
Net:	£156,000	Net:	£105,000
VAT:	£31,200	VAT:	£21,000
Gross:	£187,200	Gross:	£126,000
Sales returns day book		**Purchases returns day book**	
Net:	£3,600	Net:	£5,440
VAT:	£720	VAT:	£1,088
Gross:	£4,320	Gross:	£6,528
Cash Book			
Net cash sales:	£600		
VAT:	£120		
Gross cash sales:	£720		

(a)   **What will be the entries in the VAT control account to record the VAT transactions in the quarter?**

VAT Control

Details	Amount £	Details	Amount £

Picklist: Cash sales, Purchases, Purchases returns, Sales, Sales returns, VAT.

The VAT return has been completed and shows an amount owed to HMRC of £10,688.

(b)   **Is the VAT return correct?**   Yes/No

168 PHILIP'S CABINS

The following is an extract from Philip's Cabins books of prime entry.

	Totals for quarter	
Sales day-book	**Purchases day-book**	
Net: £179,800	Net: £100,200	
VAT: £35,960	VAT: £20,040	
Gross: £215,760	Gross: £120,240	
Sales returns day-book	**Purchases returns day-book**	
Net: £3,000	Net: £5,720	
VAT: £600	VAT: £1,144	
Gross: £3,600	Gross: £6,864	
Cash book		
Net cash sales: £560		
VAT: £112		
Gross cash sales: £672		

(a) **What will be the entries in the VAT control account to record the VAT transactions in the quarter?**

VAT control

Details	Amount £	Details	Amount £

Picklist: Cash sales, Purchases, Purchases returns, Sales, Sales returns, VAT.

The VAT return has been completed and shows an amount due to HMRC of £14,540.

(b) **Is the VAT return correct?** Yes/No

169 DISLEY

(a) **Show whether each item is a debit or credit balance in the VAT control account by copying the amount into the correct column.**

	£	Debit	Credit
VAT total in the sales day book	65,420		
VAT total in the purchases day book	21,340		
VAT total in the sales returns day book	480		
VAT balance brought forward, owed to HMRC	24,910		
VAT on irrecoverable debts	830		
VAT on petty cash expenses paid	210		

The VAT return has been completed and shows an amount due to HMRC of £67,740.

(b) **Is the VAT return correct?** Yes/No

(c) At the end of the next period, the VAT control account has debit entries amounting to £42,300 and credit entries amounting to £61,250.

The following transactions have not yet been recorded in the VAT control account:

VAT total in the discounts received day book of £980

VAT of £200 on an irrecoverable debt

What will be the balance brought down on the VAT account after the transactions above have been recorded? Also identify whether the balance will be a debit or a credit.

	£	Debit	Credit
Balance brought down			

170 KERR

(a) **Show whether each item is a debit or credit balance in the VAT control account by copying the amount into the correct column.**

	£	Debit	Credit
VAT total in the purchase returns day book	1,320		
VAT total in discounts received day book	400		
VAT on cash purchases	2,670		
VAT on the sale of equipment	970		
VAT total in discounts allowed day book	500		
VAT refund received from HMRC	2,580		
VAT on cash sales	5,880		
VAT balance brought forward, due from HMRC	2,580		

The VAT return has been completed and shows an amount due to HMRC of £5,400.

(b) **Is the VAT return correct?** Yes/No

171 NEILSON

(a) Show whether each item is a debit or credit balance in the VAT control account by copying the amount into the correct column.

	£	Debit	Credit
VAT total in the sales day book	54,670		
VAT total in the purchases day book	26,340		
VAT total in the sales returns day book	1,240		
VAT total in the purchases returns day book	760		
VAT on sale of equipment	3,210		
VAT on petty cash expenses paid	500		
VAT balance brought forward, owed to HMRC	42,180		
VAT on irrecoverable debts	430		
VAT paid to HMRC during the period	32,150		
VAT on cash sales	6,540		
VAT on cash purchases	7,520		
VAT total in discounts allowed day book	1,130		
VAT total in discounts received day book	980		

The VAT return has been completed and shows an amount due to HMRC of £39,030.

(b) **Is the VAT return correct?** Yes/No

	Balances extracted on 30 June £	Balances at 1 July	
		Debit £	Credit £
Receivables ledger control	38,070		
Payables ledger control	20,310		
VAT owed from HMRC	2,510		
Capital	70,000		
Sales	153,488		
Sales returns	2,135		
Purchases	63,261		
Purchase returns	542		
Plant and equipment	17,319		
Motor expenses	3,214		
Office expenses	6,421		
Rent and rates	17,414		
Heat and light	6,421		
Wages	45,532		
Irrecoverable debt	1,532		
Office equipment	35,313		
Bank overdraft	2,152		
Suspense account (debit balance)	7,350		
Totals			

POBC LO2 RECONCILE A BANK STATEMENT WITH THE CASH BOOK

172 BLOSSOM BLOOMS

Blossom Blooms receives payment from customers and makes payments to suppliers in a variety of ways.

(a) Select FOUR checks that DO NOT have to be made on each of the two payment methods shown below when received from customers.

Checks to be made	Cheque ✓	Telephone credit card payment ✓
Check expiry date		
Check issue number		
Check not post dated		
Check security number		
Check words and figures match		
Check card has not been tampered with		

(b) Show whether each of the statements below is true or false.

When Blossom Blooms makes payments to suppliers by debit card, the amount paid affects the bank current account.

True/False

When Blossom Blooms makes payments to suppliers by credit card, the amount paid affects the bank current account.

True/False

173 PETE'S PARROTS

Pete's Parrots receives payment from customers and makes payments to suppliers in a variety of ways.

(a) Select TWO checks that have to be made on each of the two payment methods shown below when received from customers.

Checks to be made	Cheque ✓	Telephone credit card payment ✓
Check expiry date		
Check issue number		
Check not post dated		
Check security number		
Check words and figures match		
Check card has not been tampered with		

(b) **Show whether each of the statements below is true or false.**

When Pete's Parrots makes payments to suppliers by credit card, the amount does not leave the bank current account immediately.

True/False

When Pete's Parrots makes payments to suppliers by debit card, the amount paid affects the bank current account.

True/False

174 BANK EFFECTS 1

Which TWO payments will NOT reduce funds in the bank balance of the payer at the date of payment?

	✓
Standing order	
Cheque payment	
CHAPS payment	
Credit card payment	

175 BANK EFFECTS 2

Which THREE payments WILL reduce funds in the bank balance of the payer at the date of payment?

	✓
Direct debit	
Building society cheque payment	
Debit card payment	
BACS payment	

176 METHODS OF PAYMENT 1

Match the payment need with the most likely method of payment to be used.

Replacement batteries for office clock	CHAPS payment
Payment to complete the purchase of a new building, which needs to clear today	Debit/Credit card
Fixed monthly charge for rent	Direct debit
Payment for telephone bill, which fluctuates monthly	Cheque
Payment to regular supplier	Petty cash
Online purchase of computer equipment	Standing order

177 METHODS OF PAYMENT 2

Match the payment with the description below

Standing order	A payment made for regular bills which fluctuate in value
Bank loan	A facility allowing customers to deposit cash and cheques after bank opening hours
Direct debit	A regular payment for a fixed amount
Bank overdraft	A facility allowing customers to borrow money on a long term basis
Night safe	A facility allowing customers to borrow money on a short term flexible basis

178 RIVERS LTD

The bank statement and cash book of Rivers is shown below.

Midway Bank PLC

52 The Parade, Middleton, MD1 9LA

To: Rivers Ltd   Account No: 28012877   23 June 20XX

Statement of Account

Date	Detail	Paid out	Paid in	Balance	
20XX		£	£	£	
04 June	Balance b/d			3,115	C
04 June	Cheque 101013	650		2,465	C
04 June	Cheque 101014	1,420		1,045	C
05 June	Cheque 101015	60		985	C
07 June	Cheque 101018	450		535	C
12 June	Bank Giro Credit Ayreshire Build		970	1,505	C
13 June	Cheque 101016	615		890	C
15 June	Direct debit Collins	175		715	C
19 June	Paid in at Midway bank		300	1,015	C
20 June	Direct Debit rent	500		515	C
23 June	Bank interest		15	530	C
23 June	Bank charges	20		510	C

D = Debit   C = Credit

Cash book

Date 20XX	Details	Bank £	Date 20XX	Cheque number	Details	Bank £
01 June	Balance b/d	3,115	01 June	101013	Indigo Beds	650
17 June	Bracken Ltd	300	01 June	101014	DirectFit	1,420
21 June	Airfleet Interiors	560	01 June	101015	Langdon	60
22 June	Harris Homes	333	02 June	101016	QPF Ltd	615
			03 June	101017	OMD Ltd	815
			03 June	101018	Hamden Ltd	450
			15 June	101019	Freeman and Cope	522
			15 June		Collins	175

Details columns options: Balance b/d, Balance c/d, Bank charges, QPF Ltd, Bracken Ltd, Ayreshire Build, Closing balance, Directfit, Hamden Ltd, Rent, Collins, Langdon, Airfleet Interiors, Freeman and Cope, OMD Ltd, Opening balance, Bank Interest, Indigo Beds, Harris Homes.

(a)   Check the items on the bank statement against the items in the cash book.

(b)   Enter any items in the cash book as needed.

(c)   Total the cash book and clearly show the balance carried down at 23 June (closing balance) and brought down at 24 June (opening balance).

179   LUXURY BATHROOMS

On 28 April Luxury Bathrooms received the following bank statement as at 24 April.

SKB Bank plc					
68 London Road, Reading, RG8 4RN					
To: Luxury Bathrooms	**Account No: 55548921**			**24 April 20XX**	
Statement of Account					
Date	**Detail**	**Paid out**	**Paid in**	**Balance**	
20XX		£	£	£	
03 April	Balance b/d			17,845	C
03 April	Cheque 120045	8,850		8,995	C
04 April	Bank Giro Credit Ricketts & Co		465	9,460	C
04 April	Cheque 120046	2,250		7,210	C
05 April	Cheque 120047	64		7,146	C
08 April	Cheque 120048	3,256		3,890	C
14 April	Direct Debit AMB Ltd	2,265		1,625	C
14 April	Direct Debit D Draper	2,950		1,325	D
14 April	Cheque 120050	655		1,980	D
22 April	Paid in at SKB bank		2,150	170	C
22 April	Bank charges	63		107	C
23 April	Overdraft fee	25		82	C
D = Debit C = Credit					

The cash book as at 24 April is shown below.

Cash book

Date	Details	Bank	Date	Cheque	Details	Bank
01 April	Balance b/d	17,845	01 April	120045	R Sterling Ltd	8,850
19 April	Olsen & Lane	2,150	01 April	120046	Bert Cooper	2,250
22 April	Frith Ltd	685	01 April	120047	Hetko & Sons	64
22 Aprll	Hodgetts & Co	282	02 April	120048	Barrett Ltd	3,256
			02 April	120049	K Plomer	542
			08 April	120050	I&E Brown	655
			08 April	120051	T Roberts	1,698
			14 April		AMB Ltd	2,265

Details column options: Balance b/d, balance c/d, Bank charges, R Sterling Ltd, Olsen & Lane, Frith Ltd, Hodgetts & Co, Bert Cooper, Hetko & Sons, Barrett Ltd, K Plomer, I&E Brown, T Roberts, AMB Ltd, Ricketts & Co, D Draper, Opening balance, Overdraft fees.

(a)   **Check the items on the bank statement against the items in the cash book.**

(b)   **Enter any items in the cash book as needed.**

(c)   **Total the cash book and clearly show the balance carried down at 24 April (closing balance) and brought down at 25 April (opening balance).**

180 WHOLESALE FLOORING

The bank statement and cash book for Wholesale Flooring is shown below.

Money Bags Bank PLC
52 Oak Road, Timperley, SK10 8LR

To: Wholesale Flooring	Account No: 47013799	23 June 20XX

Statement of Account

Date	Detail	Paid out	Paid in	Balance	
20XX		£	£	£	
04 June	Balance b/d			5,125	D
05 June	Cheque 104373	890		6,015	D
05 June	Cheque 104374	1,725		7,740	D
05 June	Cheque 104375	210		7,950	D
11 June	Cheque 104378	784		8,734	D
12 June	Bank Giro Credit Aintree and Co		1,250	7,484	D
13 June	Cheque 104376	1,275		8,759	D
15 June	Cheque 104377	725		9,484	D
17 June	Paid in at Money Bags Bank plc		550	8,934	D
20 June	Direct debit MD County Council	400		9,334	D
23 June	Bank charges	160		9,494	D
23 June	Overdraft fee	90		9,584	D
	D = Debit C = Credit				

Cash book

Date 20XX	Details	Bank £	Date 20XX	Cheque number	Details	Bank £
			01 June		Balance b/d	5,125
16 June	Beeston's	550	01 June	104373	Good Iron	890
19 June	Airfleet Exteriors	3,025	01 June	104374	Ashworth & Co	1,725
22 June	Jones's	2,775	01 June	104375	Ironfit	210
			05 June	104376	OSS Ltd	1,275
			07 June	104377	Perfect Tools	725
			08 June	104378	Campden Ltd	784
			14 June	104379	Thornley & Thwaite	675
			14 June	104380	Castle & Cove	178

Details columns options: Balance b/d, Balance c/d, Bank charges, Good Iron, Beeston's, Aintree & Co, Perfect Tools, Closing balance, Ashworth & Co, Thornley & Thwaite, MD County Council, Campden Ltd, Airfleet Exteriors, Castle & Cove, OSS Ltd, Opening balance, Overdraft Fee, Ironfit, Jones's.

(a) Check the items on the bank statement against the items in the cash book.

(b) Enter any items in the cash book as needed.

(c) Total the cash book and clearly show the balance carried down at 23 June (closing balance) and brought down at 24 June (opening balance).

181 24 HOUR TAXIS

On 28 June 24 Hour Taxis received the following bank statement as at 23 June.

Four Kings Bank PLC
124 Four Kings Way, Newton Mearns, GL10 5QR

To: 24 Hour Taxis   Account No: 16135844   23 June 20XX

Statement of Account

Date 20XX	Detail	Paid out £	Paid in £	Balance £	
04 June	Balance b/d			6,025	C
05 June	Cheque 102597	910		5,115	C
05 June	Cheque 102598	2,010		3,105	C
05 June	Cheque 102599	315		2,790	C
11 June	Cheque 102602	675		2,115	C
12 June	Bank Giro Credit Barron Homes		1,475	3,590	C
13 June	Cheque 102600	1,725		1,865	C
15 June	Cheque 102601	686		1,179	C
17 June	Paid in at Four Kings Bank		1,000	2,179	C
20 June	Direct Debit AB Insurance	1,250		929	C
23 June	Bank charges	50		879	C
23 June	Overdraft fee	25		854	C

D = Debit   C = Credit

Cash book

Date 20XX	Details	Bank £	Date 20XX	Cheque number	Details	Bank £
01 June	Balance b/d	6,025	01 June	102597	Best Ideas	910
18 June	Earnshaw's	1,000	02 June	102598	Bentley & Burn	2,010
19 June	Mainstreet Ltd	1,206	02 June	102599	Bits & Bats	315
21 June	Housley Inc	1,725	03 June	102600	LPF Ltd	1,725
			07 June	102601	Essentials	686
			08 June	102602	Hopburn Ltd	675
			15 June	102603	Thistle Tools	410
			15 June	102604	C Campbell Ltd	275

Details columns options: Balance b/d, Balance c/d, Bank charges, Earnshaw's, Housley Inc, C Campbell Ltd, Mainstreet Ltd, Closing balance, Barron Homes, Thistle Tools, AB Insurance, Hopburn Ltd, Best Ideas, Bentley & Burn, LPF Ltd, Opening balance, Overdraft Fee, Bits & Bats, Essentials.

(a) Check the items on the bank statement against the items in the cash book.

(b) Enter any items in the cash book as needed.

(c) Total the cash book and clearly show the balance carried down at 23 June (closing balance) and brought down at 24 June (opening balance).

182 WOOD

The bank statement and cash book for Wood is shown below.

	Money Bags Bank PLC 52 Oak Road, Timperley, SK10 8LR			
To: Wood Ltd	Account No: 47013799		23 June 20XX	

Statement of Account

Date 20XX	Detail	Paid out £	Paid in £	Balance £	
04 June	Balance b/d			17,640	C
05 June	Bank Giro Credit Bradley		1,320	18,960	C
05 June	Bank Giro Credit Thanoj		2,450	21,410	C
05 June	Paid in at Money Bags Bank PLC		9,420	30,830	C
11 June	Cheque 110341	1,540		29,290	C
12 June	BACS payment Southwell	820		28,470	C
13 June	Cheque 110343	750		27,720	C
15 June	Cheque 110344	570		27,150	C
17 June	Interest earned		80	27,230	C
20 June	Direct debit Blundell	400		26,830	C
23 June	BACS payment Bore	250		26,580	C
23 June	Cheque 110346	740		25,840	C
	D = Debit C = Credit				

Cash book

Date 20XX	Details	Bank £	Date 20XX	Cheque number	Details	Bank £
01 June	Balance b/d	17,640				
03 June	Bradley	1,320	04 June	110341	Carr	1,540
03 June	Cash sales	9,420	04 June	110342	Ramsden	980
03 June	Thanoj	2,450	04 June	110343	Coulson	750
21 June	Cash sales	7,430	04 June	110344	Brodie	570
21 June	Devitt	1,990	04 June	110345	Jones	550
			04 June	110346	Gritton	740
			20 June		Bore	250

(a) Check the items on the bank statement against the items in the cash book.

(b) Enter any items in the cash book as needed.

(c) Total the cash book and clearly show the balance carried down at 23 June (closing balance) and brought down at 24 June (opening balance).

183 PEARSON

The bank statement and cash book for Pearson is shown below:

Money Bags Bank PLC

To: Pearson Ltd | Account No: 47013799 | 23 June 20XX

Statement of Account

Date 20XX	Detail	Paid out £	Paid in £	Balance £	
01 June	Balance b/d			1,340	D
02 June	Bank Giro Credit Pond		1,890	550	C
02 June	Interest received		5	555	C
02 June	Direct Debit McMenemy	1,200		645	D
11 June	Cheque 110123	430		1,075	D
12 June	Paid in to Money Bags Bank		840	235	D
13 June	Cheque 110126	75		310	D
15 June	Cheque 110127	270		580	D
17 June	Paid in to Money Bags Bank		1,540	960	C
20 June	Direct debit Findus	300		660	C
23 June	Bank charges	25		635	C
23 June	Cheque 110129	740		105	D

D = Debit   C = Credit

Cash book

Date 20XX	Details	Bank £	Date 20XX	Cheque number	Details	Bank £
01 June	Balance b/d	550	07 June	110123	Connell	430
09 June	Cash sales	840	07 June	110124	Renner	720
14 June	Cash sales	1,540	07 June	110125	Bond	750
22 June	Cunnington	1,730	07 June	110126	Hatton	75
			07 June	110127	Bull	270
			07 June	110128	Black	135
			07 June	110129	Southall	740

(a) Check the items on the bank statement against the items in the cash book.

(b) Enter any items in the cash book as needed.

(c) Total the cash book and clearly show the balance carried down at 23 June (closing balance) and brought down at 24 June (opening balance).

184 MCKEOWN

The bank statement and cash book for McKeown is shown below.

	Money Bags Bank PLC			
To: McKeown Ltd	Account No: 47013799		23 June 20XX	

Statement of Account

Date 20XX	Detail	Paid out £	Paid in £	Balance £	
01 June	Balance b/d			7,420	C
01 June	Bank Giro Credit Pond		180	7,600	C
01 June	Cheque 110156	420		7,180	C
01 June	Interest received		85	7,265	C
11 June	Cheque 110157	430		6,835	C
12 June	Cheque 110158	520		6,315	C
13 June	Cheque 110161	750		5,565	C
15 June	Bank Giro Credit Sherwood		640	6,205	C
17 June	Paid in to Money Bags Bank		1,200	7,405	C
20 June	Bank Giro Credit Coyne		1,630	9,035	C
23 June	Direct debit Wilmott	300		8,735	C
23 June	Interest received		35	8,770	C
	D = Debit C = Credit				

Cash book

Date 20XX	Details	Bank £	Date 20XX	Cheque number	Details	Bank £
01 June	Balance b/d	7,180	07 June	110157	Williams	430
12 June	Sherwood	640	07 June	110158	Forecast	520
14 June	Cash sales	1,200	07 June	110159	Beasant	1,240
22 June	Tweedy	860	07 June	110160	Davison	1,420
23 June	Butterwood	440	07 June	110161	Mildenhall	750

(a)   Check the items on the bank statement against the items in the cash book.

(b)   Enter any items in the cash book as needed.

(c)   Total the cash book and clearly show the balance carried down at 23 June (closing balance) and brought down at 24 June (opening balance).

185 RIVERS BANK RECONCILIATION

Below is the bank statement and updated cash book for Rivers.

Midway Bank PLC					
52 The Parade, Middleton, MD1 9LA					
To: Rivers Ltd		Account No: 28012877		23 June 20XX	
Statement of Account					
Date	Detail	Paid out	Paid in	Balance	
20XX		£	£	£	
04 June	Balance b/d			3,115	C
04 June	Cheque 101013	650		2,465	C
04 June	Cheque 101014	1,420		1,045	C
05 June	Cheque 101015	60		985	C
07 June	Cheque 101018	450		535	C
12 June	Bank Giro Credit Ayreshire Build		970	1,505	C
13 June	Cheque 101016	615		890	C
15 June	Direct debit Collins	175		715	C
17 June	Paid in at Midway bank		300	1,015	C
20 June	Direct Debit rent	500		515	C
23 June	Bank interest		15	530	C
23 June	Bank charges	20		510	C
D = Debit C = Credit					

Date 20XX	Details	Bank £	Date 20XX	Cheque number	Details	Bank £
01 June	Balance b/d	3,115	01 June	101013	Indigo Beds	650
17 June	Bracken Ltd	300	01 June	101014	DirectFit	1,420
21 June	Airfleet Interiors	560	01 June	101015	Langdon	60
22 June	Harris Homes	333	01 June	101016	QPF Ltd	615
12 June	Ayreshire Build	970	02 June	101017	OMD Ltd	815
23 June	Bank Interest	15	02 June	101018	Hamden Ltd	450
			13 June	101019	Freeman & Cope	522
			13 June		Collins	175
			20 June		Rent	500
			23 June		Bank charges	20
			23 June		Balance c/d	66
		5,293				5,293
24 June	Balance b/d	66				

Complete the bank reconciliation statement as at 23 June.

Note: Do not make any entries in the shaded boxes.

Bank reconciliation statement as at 23 June 20XX

Balance per bank statement	£
Add:	
Name:	£
Name:	£
Total to add	£
Less:	
Name:	£
Name:	£
Total to subtract	£
Balance as per cash book	£

Name options: Bank charges, QPF Ltd, Bracken Ltd, Ayreshire Build, Directfit, Hamden Ltd, Rent, Collins, Langdon, Airfleet Interiors, Freeman and Cope, OMD Ltd, Bank interest, Indigo Beds, Harris homes.

186 LUXURY BATHROOMS BANK RECONCILIATION

Below is the bank statement and updated cash book for Luxury Bathrooms.

	SKB Bank plc				
	68 London Road, Reading, RG8 4RN				
To: Luxury Bathrooms	Account No: 55548921			24 April 20XX	
	Statement of Account				
Date	**Detail**	**Paid out**	**Paid in**	**Balance**	
20XX		£	£	£	
03 April	Balance b/d			17,845	C
03 April	Cheque 120045	8,850		8,995	C
04 April	Bank Giro Ricketts & Co		465	9,460	C
04 April	Cheque 120046	2,250		7,210	C
05 April	Cheque 120047	64		7,146	C
08 April	Cheque 120048	3,256		3,890	C
14 April	Direct Debit AMB Ltd	2,265		1,625	C
14 April	Direct Debit D Draper	2,950		1,325	D
14 April	Cheque 120050	655		1,980	D
22 April	Paid in at SKB Bank		2,150	170	C
22 April	Bank charges	63		107	C
23 April	Overdraft fee	25		82	C
	D = Debit C = Credit				

Date	Details	Bank	Date	Cheque	Details	Bank
01 April	Balance b/d	17,845	01 April	120045	R Sterling Ltd	8,850
19 April	Olsen & Lane	2,150	01 April	120046	Bert Cooper	2,250
22 April	Frith Ltd	685	01 April	120047	Hetko & Sons	64
22 April	Hodgetts & Co	282	02 April	120048	Barrett Ltd	3,256
04 April	Ricketts & Co	465	02 April	120049	K Plomer	542
			08 April	120050	I&E Brown	655
			08 April	120051	T Roberts	1,698
			14 April		AMB Ltd	2,265
			14 April		D Draper	2,950
			22 April		Bank charges	63
			23 April		Overdraft fee	25
24 April	Balance c/d	1,191				
		22,618				22,618
			25 April		Balance b/d	1,191

Complete the bank reconciliation statement as at **24 April.**

Note: Do not make any entries in the shaded boxes.

Bank reconciliation statement as at 24 April 20XX.

Balance per bank statement	£
Add:	
Name:	£
Name:	£
Total to add	£
Less:	
Name:	£
Name:	£
Total to subtract	£
Balance as per cash book	£

Name options: Bank charges, , R Sterling Ltd, Olsen & Lane, Frith Ltd, Hodgetts & Co, Bert Cooper, Hetko & Sons, Barrett Ltd, K Plomer, I&E Brown, T Roberts, AMB Ltd, Ricketts & Co, D Draper, Overdraft fee.

187 WHOLESALE FLOORING BANK RECONCILIATION

Below is the bank statement and updated cash book for Wholesale Flooring.

Money Bags Bank PLC
52 Oak Road, Timperley, SK10 8LR

To: Wholesale Flooring   Account No: 47013799   23 June 20XX
Statement of Account

Date 20XX	Detail	Paid out £	Paid in £	Balance £	
04 June	Balance b/d			5,125	D
05 June	Cheque 104373	890		6,015	D
05 June	Cheque 104374	1,725		7,740	D
05 June	Cheque 104375	210		7,950	D
11 June	Cheque 104378	784		8,734	D
12 June	Bank Giro Credit Aintree and Co		1,250	7,484	D
13 June	Cheque 104376	1,275		8,759	D
15 June	Cheque 104377	725		9,484	D
17 June	Paid in at Money Bags Bank plc		550	8,934	D
20 June	Direct debit MD County Council	400		9,334	D
23 June	Bank charges	160		9,494	D
23 June	Overdraft fee	90		9,584	D

D = Debit   C = Credit

Date 20XX	Details	Bank £	Date 20XX	Cheque number	Details	Bank £
			01 June		Balance b/d	5,125
16 June	Beeston's	550	01 June	104373	Good Iron	890
19 June	Airfleet Exteriors	3,025	01 June	104374	Ashworth & Co	1,725
22 June	Jones's	2,775	01 June	104375	Ironfit	210
12 June	Aintree & Co	1,250	05 June	104376	OSS Ltd	1,275
			07 June	104377	Perfect Tools	725
			08 June	104378	Campden Ltd	784
			14 June	104379	Thornley & Thwaite	675
			14 June	104380	Castle and Cove	178
			20 June		MD County Council	400
			23 June		Bank charges	160
23 June	Balance c/d	4,637	23 June		Overdraft fee	90
		12,237				12,237
			24 June		Balance b/d	4,637

Complete the bank reconciliation statement as at 23 June.

Note: Do not make any entries in the shaded boxes.

Bank reconciliation statement as at 23 June 20XX

Balance per bank statement	£
Add:	
Name:	£
Name:	£
Total to add	£
Less:	
Name:	£
Name:	£
Total to subtract	£
Balance as per cash book	£

Name options: Bank charges, OSS Ltd, Beeston's, Aintree and Co, Ironfit, Campden Ltd, MD County Council, Ashworth & Co, Airfleet Exteriors, Thornley & Thwaite, Perfect Tools, Overdraft fee, Castle & Cove, Good Iron, Jones's.

188 24 HOUR TAXIS BANK RECONCILIATION

Below is the bank statement and updated cash book for 24 Hour Taxis.

Four Kings Bank PLC
124 Four Kings Way, Newton Mearns, GL10 5QR

To: 24 Hour Taxis   Account No: 16135844   23 June 20XX

Statement of Account

Date	Detail	Paid out	Paid in	Balance	
20XX		£	£	£	
04 June	Balance b/d			6,025	C
05 June	Cheque 102597	910		5,115	C
05 June	Cheque 102598	2,010		3,105	C
05 June	Cheque 102599	315		2,790	C
11 June	Cheque 102602	675		2,115	C
12 June	Bank Giro credit Barron Homes		1,475	3,590	C
13 June	Cheque 102600	1,725		1,865	C
15 June	Cheque 102601	686		1,179	C
18 June	Paid in at Four Kings Bank		1,000	2,179	C
20 June	Direct Debit AB Insurance	1,250		929	C
23 June	Bank charges	50		879	C
23 June	Overdraft fee	25		854	C
D = Debit C = Credit					

Date 20XX	Details	Bank £	Date 20XX	Cheque number	Details	Bank £
01 June	Balance b/d	6,025	01 June	102597	Best ideas	910
18 June	Earnshaw's	1,000	02 June	102598	Bentley and Burn	2,010
19 June	Mainstreet Ltd	1,206	02 June	102599	Bits and Bats	315
21 June	Housley Inc	1,725	03 June	102600	LPF Ltd	1,725
12 June	Barron Homes	1,475	07 June	102601	Essentials	686
			08 June	102602	Hopburn Ltd	675
			15 June	102603	Thistle Tools	410
			15 June	102604	C Campbell Ltd	275
			20 June		AB Insurance	1,250
			23 June		Bank charges	50
			23 June		Overdraft fee	25
			23 June		Balance c/d	3,100
		11,431				11,431
24 June	Balance b/d	3,100				

Complete the bank reconciliation statement as at 23 June.

Note: Do not make any entries in the shaded boxes.

Bank reconciliation statement as at 23 June 20XX

Balance per bank statement	£
Add:	
Name:	£
Name:	£
Total to add	£
Less:	
Name:	£
Name:	£
Total to subtract	£
Balance as per cash book	£

Name options: Bank charges, LPF Ltd, Earnshaw's, Barron Homes, Best Ideas, C Campbell Ltd, AB Insurance, Housley Inc, Mainstreet Ltd, Thistle Tools, Bentley and Burn, Overdraft fee, Hopburn Ltd, Bits & Bats, Essentials.

189   WOOD BANK RECONCILIATION

The bank statement and cash book for Wood is shown below.

Money Bags Bank PLC
52 Oak Road, Timperley, SK10 8LR

To: Wood Ltd   Account No: 47013799   23 June 20XX

Statement of Account

Date	Detail	Paid out	Paid in	Balance	
20XX		£	£	£	
04 June	Balance b/d			17,640	C
05 June	Bank Giro Credit Bradley		1,320	18,960	C
05 June	Bank Giro Credit Thanoj		2,450	21,410	C
05 June	Paid in at Money Bags Bank PLC		9,420	30,830	C
11 June	Cheque 110341	1,540		29,290	C
12 June	BACS payment Southwell	820		28,470	C
13 June	Cheque 110343	750		27,720	C
15 June	Cheque 110344	570		27,150	C
17 June	Interest earned		80	27,230	C
20 June	Direct Debit Blundell	400		26,830	C
23 June	BACS payment Bore	250		26,580	C
23 June	Cheque 110346	740		25,840	C
	D = Debit C = Credit				

Cash book

Date 20XX	Details	Bank £	Date 20XX	Cheque number	Details	Bank £
01 June	Balance b/d	17,640				
03 June	Bradley	1,320	04 June	110341	Carr	1,540
03 June	Cash sales	9,420	04 June	110342	Ramsden	980
03 June	Thanoj	2,450	04 June	110343	Coulson	750
21 June	Cash sales	7,430	04 June	110344	Brodie	570
21 June	Devitt	1,990	04 June	110345	Jones	550
17 June	Interest earned	80	04 June	110346	Gritton	740
			20 June		Bore	250
			12 June		Southwell	820
			20 June		Direct Debit Blundell	400

(a) **Complete the bank reconciliation statement as at 23 June.**

Note: Do not make any entries in the shaded boxes.

Bank reconciliation statement as at 23 June 20XX

Balance per bank statement	
Add:	
Name:	
Name:	
Total to add	
Less:	
Name:	
Name:	
Total to subtract	
Balance as per cash book	

(b) Refer to the cash book in (a) and check that the bank statement has correctly been reconciled by calculating:

− The balance carried down

− The total of each of the bank columns after the balance carried down has been recorded

Balance carried down £	Bank column totals £

190   PEARSON BANK RECONCILIATION

The bank statement and cash book for Pearson is shown below.

Money Bags Bank PLC

To: Pearson Ltd   Account No: 47013799   23 June 20XX

Statement of Account

Date	Detail	Paid out	Paid in	Balance	
20XX		£	£	£	
01 June	Balance b/d			1,340	D
02 June	Bank Giro Credit Pond		1,890	550	C
02 June	Interest received		5	555	C
02 June	Direct Debit McMenemy	1,200		645	D
11 June	Cheque 110123	430		1,075	D
12 June	Paid in to Money Bags Bank		840	235	D
13 June	Cheque 110126	75		310	D
15 June	Cheque 110127	270		580	D
17 June	Paid in to Money Bags bank		1,540	960	C
20 June	Direct Debit Findus	300		660	C
23 June	Bank charges	25		635	C
23 June	Cheque 110129	740		105	D
	D = Debit C = Credit				

Cash book

Date 20XX	Details	Bank £	Date 20XX	Cheque number	Details	Bank £
01 June	Balance b/d	550	07 June	110123	Connell	430
09 June	Cash sales	840	07 June	110124	Renner	720
14 June	Cash sales	1,540	07 June	110125	Bond	750
22 June	Cunnington	1,730	07 June	110126	Hatton	75
02 June	Interest received	5	07 June	110127	Bull	270
			07 June	110128	Black	135
			07 June	110129	Southall	740
			02 June		McMenemy	1,200
			20 June		Findus	300
			23 June		Bank charges	25
			23 June		Balance c/d	20
		4,665				4,665
24 June	Balance b/d	20				

(a) **Complete the bank reconciliation statement as at 23 June.**

Note: Do not make any entries in the shaded boxes.

Bank reconciliation statement as at 23 June 20XX

Balance per bank statement	
Add:	
Name:	
Total to add	
Less:	
Name:	
Name:	
Name:	
Total to subtract	
Balance as per cash book	

(b) **Show which security procedure listed below Pearson should use to ensure the security of receipts from customers.**

	✓
Cash received from customers should be kept in a locked safe until banked	
Cash should be banked on a monthly basis	
Cheques received too late to bank should be posted through the bank's letter box	

191 MCKEOWN BANK RECONCILIATION

The bank statement and cash book for McKeown is shown below.

Money Bags Bank PLC

To: McKeown Ltd   Account No: 47013799   23 June 20XX

Statement of Account

Date	Detail	Paid out	Paid in	Balance	
20XX		£	£	£	
01 June	Balance b/d			7,420	C
01 June	Bank Giro Credit Pond		180	7,600	C
01 June	Cheque 110156	420		7,180	C
01 June	Interest received		85	7,265	C
11 June	Cheque 110157	430		6,835	C
12 June	Cheque 110158	520		6,315	C
13 June	Cheque 110161	750		5,565	C
15 June	Bank Giro Credit Sherwood		640	6,205	C
17 June	Paid in to Money Bags Bank		1,200	7,405	C
20 June	Bank Giro Credit Coyne		1,630	9,035	C
23 June	Direct Debit Wilmott	300		8,735	C
23 June	Interest received		35	8,770	C
	D = Debit C = Credit				

Cash book

Date 20XX	Details	Bank £	Date 20XX	Cheque number	Details	Bank £
01 June	Balance b/d	7,180	07 June	110157	Williams	430
12 June	Sherwood	640	07 June	110158	Forecast	520
14 June	Cash sales	1,200	07 June	110159	Beasant	1,240
22 June	Tweedy	860	07 June	110160	Davison	1,420
23 June	Butterwood	440	07 June	110161	Mildenhall	750
01 June	Interest received	85	23 June		Wilmott	300
20 June	Coyne	1,630				
23 June	Interest received	35				

(a)   Complete the bank reconciliation statement as at 23 June.

Note: Do not make any entries in the shaded boxes.

Bank reconciliation statement as at 23 June 20XX

Balance per bank statement	
Add:	
Name:	
Name:	
Total to add	
Less:	
Name:	
Name:	
Total to subtract	
Balance as per cash book	

(b)   Refer to the cash book in (a) and check that the bank statement has correctly been reconciled by calculating:

–   the balance carried down

–   the total of each of the bank columns after the balance carried down has been recorded.

Balance carried down £	Bank column totals £

POBC L03 USE THE JOURNAL

192 INTREPID INTERIORS

(a) Intrepid Interiors has started a new business, Intrepid Exteriors, and a new set of accounts are to be opened. A partially completed journal to record the opening entries is shown below.

Record the journal entries needed in the accounts in the general ledger of Intrepid Exteriors to deal with the opening entries.

Account name	Amount £	Debit ✓	Credit ✓
Cash at bank	7,250		
Bank loan	5,000		
Capital	10,625		
Motor vehicles	4,750		
Insurances	575		
Stationery	300		
Sundry expenses	225		
Motor expenses	135		
Advertising	990		
Rent and rates	1,400		
Journal to record the opening entries of new business			

(b) **From the list below, select which one of the following transactions would be recorded in the journal.**

Picklist: Credit sale, contra, electricity expense, reimbursement of petty cash

193 BEDROOM BITS

(a) Record the journal entries needed in the accounts in the general ledger of Bedroom Bits to show if each item is a debit or credit.

Account name	Amount £	Debit ✓	Credit ✓
Cash	325		
Cash at bank	9,625		
Capital	22,008		
Fixtures and fittings	4,250		
Insurance	1,050		
Loan from bank	15,000		
Miscellaneous expenses	413		
Motor vehicle	19,745		
Office expenses	350		
Rent and rates	1,250		

(b) From the list below, select which one of the following transactions would be recorded in the journal.

Picklist: Prompt payment discount given, the return of goods to a supplier, interest received from the bank, irrecoverable debt written off

194 GARDEN GATES

Record the journal entries in the general ledger of Garden Gates to show if each item is a debit or a credit

Account name	Amount £	Debit ✓	Credit ✓
Cash	450		
Cash at bank	11,125		
Capital	26,248		
Plant and machinery	5,050		
Insurance	990		
Loan from bank	12,500		
General office expenses	378		
Motor vehicle	20,755		

195 IVANO

Ivano's pay details for June are listed below:

Transaction	Amount £
Gross pay	2,400
PAYE	480
Employee's NIC	245
Employee's contribution to pension	80
Employer's NIC	255

Fill in the boxes required below:

(a)

	Amount £
Net pay	

(b)

	Amount £
Wages and salaries (Employer's expense)	

(c)

	Amount £
Liabilities (HMRC and pension)	

196 ANNA

Anna's pay details for June are listed below:

Transaction	Amount £
Gross pay	1,400
PAYE	280
Employee's NIC	125
Employer's contribution to pension	70
Employee's contribution to pension	60
Employer's NIC	135

Fill in the boxes required below:

(a)

	Amount £
Net pay	

(b)

	Amount £
Wages and salaries (Employer's expense)	

(c)

	Amount £
Liabilities (HMRC and pension)	

197 GROSS PAY 1

Which of the items listed below would be added to an employee's gross pay to calculate the total wages expense?

Item	Added to gross pay ✓	Not added to gross pay ✓
Trade Union subscription		
Employer's NIC		
Employee's Pension		
Employer's Pension		
Employee's NIC		

198 GROSS PAY 2

Which of the items listed below would be deducted from an employee's gross pay to calculate net pay?

Item	Deducted from gross pay ✓	Not deducted from gross pay ✓
Employer's NIC		
Commission		
Employee's NIC		
Employee pension contribution		
PAYE		

199 A POCKET FULL OF POSES

A Pocket Full of Poses pays its employees by cheque every month and maintains a wages control account. A summary of last month's payroll transactions is shown below:

Item	£
Gross wages	15,000
Employers' NI	1,755
Employees' NI	1,410
Income tax	4,335
Employers' pension contributions	1,000
Employees' pension contributions	850

Record the journal entries needed in the general ledger to:

(i)   Record the wages expense

(ii)   Record the HMRC liability

(iii) Record the net wages paid to the employees

(iv)   Record the pension liability.

(i)

Account name	Amount £	Debit ✓	Credit ✓

(ii)

Account name	Amount £	Debit ✓	Credit ✓

(iii)

Account name	Amount £	Debit ✓	Credit ✓

(iv)

Account name	Amount £	Debit ✓	Credit ✓

Picklist for each: Bank, Employees NI, Employers NI, HMRC, Income tax, Net wages, Pension, Trade union, Wages control, Wages expense.

200 RHYME TIME

Rhyme Time pays its employees by cheque every month and maintains a wages control account. A summary of last month's payroll transactions is shown below:

Item	£
Gross wages	10,130
Employers' NI	1,185
Employees' NI	1,006
Income tax	2,835
Employers' pension contributions	600
Employees' pension contributions	550

Record the journal entries needed in the general ledger to:

(i)   **Record the wages expense**

(ii)   **Record the HMRC liability**

(iii)   **Record the net wages paid to the employees**

(iv)   **Record the pension liability.**

(i)

Account name	Amount £	Debit ✓	Credit ✓

(ii)

Account name	Amount £	Debit ✓	Credit ✓

(iii)

Account name	Amount £	Debit ✓	Credit ✓

(iv)

Account name	Amount £	Debit ✓	Credit ✓

201 DOWN & OUT

Down & Out pays it employees by cheque every month and maintains a wages control account. A summary of last month's payroll transactions is shown below:

Item	£
Gross wages	8,542
Employers' NI	1,025
Employees' NI	940
Income tax	1,708
Trade union fees	425

Record the journal entries needed in the general ledger to:

(i)   **Record the wages expense**

(ii)   **Record the HMRC liability**

(iii)   **Record the net wages paid to the employees**

(iv)   **Record the trade union liability.**

(i)

Account name	Amount £	Debit ✓	Credit ✓

(ii)

Account name	Amount £	Debit ✓	Credit ✓

(iii)

Account name	Amount £	Debit ✓	Credit ✓

(iv)

Account name	Amount £	Debit ✓	Credit ✓

Picklist for each: Bank, Employees NI, Employers NI, HMRC, Income Tax, Net wages, Trade union, Wages control, Wages expense.

202 DEV

Dev pays its employees by cheque every month and maintains a wages control account. A summary of last month's payroll transactions is shown below:

Item	£
Gross wages	12,500
Employers' NI	1,463
Employees' NI	1,175
Income tax	3,613
Trade union fees	500

Record the journal entries needed in the general ledger to:

(i)   Record the wages expense

(ii)   Record the HMRC liability

(iii) Record the net wages paid to the employees

(iv) Record the trade union liability.

(i)

Account name	Amount £	Debit ✓	Credit ✓

(ii)

Account name	Amount £	Debit ✓	Credit ✓

(iii)

Account name	Amount £	Debit ✓	Credit ✓

(iv)

Account name	Amount £	Debit ✓	Credit ✓

Picklist for each: Bank, Employees NI, Employers NI, HMRC, Income tax, Net wages, Pension, Trade union, Wages control, Wages expense.

203 BEDROOM BITS

A credit customer, ABC Ltd, has ceased trading, owing Bedroom Bits £2,400 including VAT.

Record the journal entries needed in the general ledger to write off the net amount and the VAT.

Account name	Amount £	Debit ✓	Credit ✓

Picklist: Irrecoverable debts, ABC Ltd, Bedroom Bits, Purchases, Payables ledger control, Sales, Receivables ledger control, VAT.

204 GARDEN GATES

A credit customer, A B Landscapes Ltd, has ceased trading, owing Garden Gates £2,600 plus VAT at 20%.

Record the journal entries needed in the general ledger to write off the net amount and the VAT.

Account name	Amount £	Debit ✓	Credit ✓

Picklist: Irrecoverable debts, A B Landscapes Ltd, Garden Gates, Purchases, Payables ledger control, Sales, Receivables ledger control, VAT.

205 CHESTNUT

On 1 December Chestnut had a balance of £46,000 on its Receivables Ledger Control Account and £31,000 on its Payables Ledger Control Account. It sold goods to Cook, one of its main suppliers, and was owed £4,000 by Cook at 1 December. Cook was owed £12,000 for goods it had sold to Chestnut.

Perform a contra and balance off the ledger accounts below. Dates are not required.

RLCA

Details	Amount £	Details	Amount £

PLCA

Details	Amount £	Details	Amount £

206 ALLEN

On 1 December Allen had a balance of £49,000 on its PLCA and £56,000 on its RLCA. It purchased goods from Dulieu, one of its main customers, and owed Dulieu £11,000 at 1 December. Dulieu owed Allen £23,000 for goods it had purchased from Allen.

Perform a contra and balance off the ledger accounts below. Dates are not required.

RLCA

Details	Amount £	Details	Amount £

PLCA

Details	Amount £	Details	Amount £

207 BEANZ

This is a customer's account in the receivables ledger.

Beanz Co

Details	Amount £	Details	Amount £
Balance b/f	4,530	Payment received	2,100
Invoice SD4564	3,210	Credit note	420

The customer has now ceased trading.

Record the journal entries needed to write off the receivable in the general ledger including VAT.

Account name	Amount £	Debit ✓	Credit ✓

Picklist: Irrecoverable debts, Beanz Co, Purchases, Payables ledger control, Sales, Receivables ledger control, VAT.

208 ERROR TYPES 1

Show which of the errors below are, or are not, disclosed by the trial balance.

Error in the general ledger	Error disclosed by the trial balance ✓	Error NOT disclosed by the trial balance ✓
Incorrectly calculating the balance on the Motor Vehicles account.		
Recording a receipt for commission received in the bank interest received account.		
Recording a bank receipt for bank interest received on the debit side of both the bank account and the bank interest received account.		
Recording supplier invoices on the debit side of the payables ledger control account and the credit side of the purchases account		
Recording a payment by cheque to a payable in the payables ledger control account only.		
Recording a bank payment of £124 for insurance as £142 in the insurance account and £124 in the bank account.		

209 ERROR TYPES 2

Show which of the errors below would cause an imbalance in the trial balance.

Error in the general ledger	Would cause imbalance ✓	Would NOT cause imbalance ✓
Recording a bank receipt for rent received on the credit side of both the bank account and rent received account.		
Recording a payment for new machinery in the equipment hire account.		
Recording a purchase return on the credit side of the payables ledger control account and the debit side of the purchase returns account.		
Incorrectly calculating the balance on the bank interest received account.		
Recording a payment by cheque to a payable in the bank account only.		
Recording a bank payment of £120 for stationery as £210 in both accounts.		

210 ERROR TYPES 3

Match each error description with the correct type of error by placing the appropriate answer in the table below.

Error in the general ledger	Type of error
Recording a bank receipt for rent received on the credit side of both the bank account and rent received account.	
Recording a payment for new machinery in the equipment hire account.	
Recording a purchase return on the credit side of the PLCA and the debit side of the purchase returns account.	

Picklist: Transposition error, compensating error, error of original entry, error of omission, error of commission, error of principle, reversal of entries, casting error, single entry, extraction error, two entries on one side

211 ERROR TYPES 4

Match each error description with the correct type of error by placing the appropriate answer in the table below.

Error in the general ledger	Type of error
Recording a payment to a payable in the bank account only.	
Recording a bank payment of £100 for stationery as £210 in both accounts.	
Recording a receipt for commission received in the bank interest received account.	

Picklist for all above: Transposition error, compensating error, error of original entry, error of omission, error of commission, error of principle, reversal of entries, casting error, single entry, extraction error, two entries on one side

212 ERROR TYPES 5

Match each error description with the correct type of error by placing the appropriate answer in the table below.

Error in the general ledger	Type of error
A credit sale made at the month end was not recorded.	
Recording a bank payment of £120 for stationery as £210 in the stationery account and correctly in the bank account.	
Recording a receipt for commission received in the PLCA.	

Picklist for all above: Transposition error, compensating error, error of original entry, error of omission, error of commission, error of principle, reversal of entries, casting error, single entry, extraction error, two entries on one side

213 ERROR TYPES 6

Show which of the errors below would cause an imbalance in the trial balance.

Error in the general ledger	Would cause imbalance ✓
Forgetting to post a journal to record a contra.	
Posting the VAT on a sale transaction as a debit rather than a credit.	
Recording a cash purchase in purchases and VAT only.	
Recording the electricity expense as a debit to wages expenses, with the corresponding entry correctly credited to cash.	

214 PRINCIPLES

(a) **Show which error is an error of principle.**

Error in the general ledger	✓
Incorrectly totalling up the sales day book.	
Recording a bank payment for rent on the debit side of the office equipment account.	
Recording rent received as a debit entry in the rent and rates account.	
Recording a payment to a supplier in the payables ledger only.	

(b) **Show which error represents two entries on one side.**

Error in the general ledger	✓
Incorrectly totalling up the sales day book.	
Recording a bank payment for rent on the debit side of the office equipment account.	
Recording rent received as a debit entry in the rent and rates account.	
Recording a payment to a supplier in the payables ledger only.	

215 EXTRACTION

(a) **Show which error is an error of extraction.**

Error in the general ledger	✓
Incorrectly totalling up the sales day book.	
Totalling the sales day book correctly but entering the total into the RLCA as a credit balance.	
Recording drawings as a debit to drawings and a credit to cash.	
Forgetting to post the entries for payroll.	

(b) **Show which error represents an error of original entry.**

Error in the general ledger	✓
Posting a £210 invoice for electricity as £210 in the electricity account but £120 in the bank account.	
Posting an invoice for electricity as a debit in both the electricity and bank accounts.	
Posting electricity expense as a credit to electricity and a debit to the bank account.	
Posting a £200 invoice for electricity as £210 in both the electricity and bank account.	

216 BANK ERROR

An entry to record a bank payment of £750 for repairs has been reversed.

Record the journal entries needed in the general ledger to

(i) **remove the incorrect entry**

(ii) **record the correct entry.**

(i)

Account name	Amount £	Debit ✓	Credit ✓

(ii)

Account name	Amount £	Debit ✓	Credit ✓

Picklist for all above: Bank, Cash, Rent, Purchases, Payables ledger control, Repairs, Sales, Receivables ledger control, Suspense, VAT.

217   RENT ERROR

An entry to record a bank receipt of £500 for rent received has been reversed.

Record the journal entries needed in the general ledger to:

(i)   remove the incorrect entry

(ii)   record the correct entry.

(i)

Account name	Amount £	Debit ✓	Credit ✓

(ii)

Account name	Amount £	Debit ✓	Credit ✓

Picklist for all above: Bank, Cash, Rent Received, Purchases, Payables ledger control, Sales, Receivables ledger control, Suspense, VAT.

218   GAS ERROR

An entry to record a gas expense of £300 was made correctly in the bank but was posted to electricity expenses instead of gas expenses.

Record the journal entries needed in the general ledger to record the correction.

Account name	Amount £	Debit ✓	Credit ✓

219   BUILDING ERROR

An entity purchased a new building for £400,000. This amount was debited to the buildings account, but £40,000 was credited to the bank account, requiring the creation of a suspense account.

Record the journal entries needed in the general ledger to record the correction.

Account name	Amount £	Debit ✓	Credit ✓

220 SALES ERROR

A credit sale of £12,000 including VAT at 20% has been made. The full £12,000 has been debited to the RLCA and credited to sales.

Record the journal entries needed in the general ledger to record the correction.

Account name	Amount £	Debit ✓	Credit ✓

221 MOTOR ERROR

An entity incurred costs of £700 to repair a motor vehicle, which it has debited to the motor vehicles account.

Record the journal entries needed in the general ledger to record the correction.

Account name	Amount £	Debit ✓	Credit ✓

222 INVENTORY ERROR

An entity purchased goods for £720 including VAT at 20%, but recorded the purchase as £270 including VAT in the purchase day book.

Record the journal entries needed in the general ledger to record the correction.

Account name	Amount £	Debit ✓	Credit ✓

223 SUBSCRIPTIONS ERROR

A junior member of the accounts team has processed the monthly bank payment of £80 for subscriptions by debiting the bank account and crediting the subscriptions account.

Record the journal entries needed in the general ledger to record the correction.

Account name	Amount £	Debit ✓	Credit ✓

224 PURCHASE ERROR

A credit purchase of £9,000 including VAT at 20% has been made. The full £9,000 has been debited to purchases and credited to the payables ledger control account.

Record the journal entries needed in the general ledger to record the correction.

Account name	Amount £	Debit ✓	Credit ✓

225 INSURANCE ERROR

A payment for insurance of £2,700 has been made. The correct amount has been debited to the insurance expense account and credited to the payables ledger control account.

Record the journal entries needed in the general ledger to record the correction.

Account name	Amount £	Debit ✓	Credit ✓

226 CB INTERIORS

CB Interiors' initial trial balance includes a suspense account with a balance of £8,640.

The error has been traced to the purchase day-book shown below.

Purchase day-book

Date	Details	Invoice number	Total £	VAT £	Net £
30 Jun	Able Paints Ltd	2763	2,400	400	2,000
30 Jun	Matley Materials	2764	3,120	520	2,600
30 Jun	Teesdale Parts	2765	4,080	680	3,400
	Totals		960	1,600	8,000

Identify the error and record the journal entries needed in the general ledger to

(i)   remove the incorrect entry

(ii)   record the correct entry

(iii) remove the suspense account balance.

(i)

Account name	Amount £	Debit ✓	Credit ✓

(ii)

Account name	Amount £	Debit ✓	Credit ✓

(iii)

Account name	Amount £	Debit ✓	Credit ✓

Picklist for all above: Able Paints Ltd, Matley Materials, Teesdale Parts, Purchases, Purchases day-book, Payables ledger control, Purchases returns, Purchases returns day-book, Sales, Sales day-book, Receivables ledger control, Sales returns, Sales returns day-book, Suspense, VAT.

227 ROGER DODGER

Roger Dodger's initial trial balance includes a suspense account with a balance of £360.

The error has been traced to the purchase returns day-book shown below.

Purchase returns day-book

DATE 20XX	Details	Note number	Total £	VAT £	Net £
30 Jun	Dennis Designs Ltd	421	1,200	200	1,000
30 Jun	XYZ Ltd	422	1,920	320	1,600
30 Jun	Denby Prints	423	4,800	800	4,000
	Totals		7,920	1,680	6,600

Identify the error and record the journal entries needed in the general ledger to:

(i)   remove the incorrect entry

(ii)   record the correct entry

(iii) remove the suspense account balance.

(i)

Account name	Amount £	Debit ✓	Credit ✓

(ii)

Account name	Amount £	Debit ✓	Credit ✓

(iii)

Account name	Amount £	Debit ✓	Credit ✓

Picklist for all above: Dennis Designs Ltd, XYZ Ltd, Denby Prints, Purchases, Purchases day-book, Payables ledger control, Purchases returns, Purchases returns day-book, Sales, Sales day-book, Receivables ledger control, Sales returns, Sales returns day-book, Suspense, VAT.

228 A CUT ABOVE

A Cut Above's initial trial balance includes a suspense account with a balance of £230.

The error has been traced to the purchase returns day-book shown below.

Purchases returns day-book

Date 20XX	Details	Returns note number	Total £	VAT £	Net £
30 April	A & S Timber Ltd	12 – 356K	576	96	480
30 April	GB Tools	AB768 – 2	816	136	680
30 April	LAH Ltd	236	4,560	760	3,800
	Totals		6,182	992	4,960

Identify the error and record the journal entries needed in the general ledger to:

(i)   remove the incorrect entry

(ii)   record the correct entry

(iii)   remove the suspense account balance.

(i)

Account name	Amount £	Debit ✓	Credit ✓

(ii)

Account name	Amount £	Debit ✓	Credit ✓

(iii)

Account name	Amount £	Debit ✓	Credit ✓

Picklist for all above: A & S Timber Ltd, GB Tools, LAH Ltd, Purchases, Purchases day-book, Payables ledger control, Purchases returns, Purchase returns day-books, Sales, Sales day-book, Receivables ledger control, Sales returns, Sales returns day-books, Suspense, VAT.

229 RESTCO

Restco's initial trial balance includes a suspense account with a balance of £720.

The error has been traced to the sales day-book shown below.

Sales day-book

Date 20XX	Details	Invoice number	Total £	VAT £	Net £
30 Jun	Ben's Build Ltd	11232	2,160	360	1,800
30 Jun	OPP Ltd	11233	3,360	560	2,800
30 Jun	Outside Capers	11234	5,040	840	4,200
	Totals		10,560	1,760	8,080

Identify the error and record the journal entries needed in the general ledger to

(i) **remove the incorrect entry**

(ii) **record the correct entry**

(iii) **remove the suspense account balance.**

(i)

Account name	Amount £	Debit ✓	Credit ✓

(ii)

Account name	Amount £	Debit ✓	Credit ✓

(iii)

Account name	Amount £	Debit ✓	Credit ✓

Picklist for all above: Ben's Build Ltd, OPP Ltd, Outside Capers, Purchases, Purchases day-book, Payables ledger control, Purchases returns, Purchases returns day-book, Sales, Sales day-book, Receivables ledger control, Sales returns, Sales returns day-book, Suspense, VAT.

230 JOHNNY JOINER

Johnny Joiner's trial balance was extracted and did not balance. The debit column of the trial balance totalled £442,735 and the credit column totalled £428,372.

(a) **What entry would be made in the suspense account to balance the trial balance?**

Account name	Amount £	Debit ✓	Credit ✓
Suspense			

(b) The error has been traced to sales, which were posted as £241,874 instead of £256,237.

Record the journal entries needed in the general ledger to record the correction.

Account name	Amount £	Debit ✓	Credit ✓

231 BUCKLEY DRAINS

Buckley Drains' trial balance was extracted and did not balance. The debit column of the trial balance totalled £336,728 and the credit column totalled £325,923.

(a) **What entry would be made in the suspense account to balance the trial balance?**

Account name	Amount £	Debit ✓	Credit ✓
Suspense			

(b) The error has been traced to an unpaid invoice for advertising, which was recorded correctly in advertising expenses but nowhere else.

Record the journal entries needed in the general ledger to record the correction.

Account name	Amount £	Debit ✓	Credit ✓

(c) **Show one reason for maintaining the journal**

	✓
To correct errors only	
To correct errors and record transactions that have not been recorded in any other book of prime entry	
To record transactions from every other book of prime entry.	

232 MENDONCA

Mendonca's trial balance was extracted and did not balance. The debit column of the trial balance totalled £643,475 and the credit column totalled £641,495

(a) **What entry would be made in the suspense account to balance the trial balance?**

Account name	Amount £	Debit ✓	Credit ✓

(b) The error has been traced to the posting of the wages payment. The total payment made was £3,200. This was incorrectly made in both the wages and bank account. The amount recorded in wages was £2,300, with a credit made to the bank of £320.

Record the journal entries needed in the general ledger to record the correction.

Account name	Amount £	Debit ✓	Credit ✓

233 BEASANT

Beasant's trial balance was extracted and did not balance. The debit column of the trial balance totalled £630,000 and the credit column totalled £615,000.

(a) **What entry would be made in the suspense account to balance the trial balance?**

Account name	Amount £	Debit ✓	Credit ✓
Suspense			

(b) The error has been traced to a late credit sale. The full amount of the sale (including VAT at 20%) was correctly recorded in the RLCA but no other entries were made.

Record the journal entries needed in the general ledger to record the correction.

Account name	Amount £	Debit ✓	Credit ✓

(c)   Show one reason for maintaining the journal

	✓
To detect fraud	
To record non-regular transactions	
To record goods sold on credit	

234   PAT'S CAFE

Pat's Cafe's trial balance did not balance. The debit column totalled £67,410 and the credit column totalled £72,060.

(a)   **What entry would be made in the suspense account to balance the trial balance?**

Account name	Amount £	Debit ✓	Credit ✓

The journal entries to correct the bookkeeping errors, and a list of balances as they appear in the trial balance, are shown below.

Journal entries

Account name	Debit £	Credit £
Bank interest paid	114	
Bank interest received		114
Insurance	150	
Suspense		150
Motor vehicles	4,500	
Suspense		4,500

Account name

Account name	Debit £	Credit £
Bank interest paid	121	
Bank interest received	53	
Insurance	400	
Motor vehicles	2000	

(b)   Complete the table below to show the new balances, and whether each will be a debit or a credit.

Account name	Balance £	Debit ✓	Credit ✓
Bank interest paid			
Bank interest received			
Insurance			
Motor vehicles			

235 TWINKLE'S TRINKETS

Twinkle's Trinkets trial balance did not balance. The debit column totalled £112,340 and the credit column totalled £111,564.

(a)   What entry would be made in the suspense account to balance the trial balance?

Account name	Amount £	Debit ✓	Credit ✓
Suspense			

The journal entries to correct the bookkeeping errors, and a list of balances as they appear in the trial balance, are shown below.

Journal entries

Account name	Debit £	Credit £
Motor expenses	324	
Suspense		324
Suspense	1,100	
Repairs and renewals		1,100
Rent payable	500	
Rent received		500

Account name

Account name	Debit £	Credit £
Motor expenses	8,420	
Repairs and renewals	2,310	
Rent payable	3,200	
Rent received		1,200

(b) **Complete the table below to show the new balances, and whether each will be a debit or a credit.**

Account name	Balance £	Debit ✓	Credit ✓
Motor expenses			
Repairs and renewals			
Rent payable			
Rent received			

236 SPARKS AND MENCER

Sparks and Mencer's trial balance included a suspense account. All the bookkeeping errors have now been traced and the journal entries shown below have been recorded.

The journal entries to correct the bookkeeping errors, and a list of balances as they appear in the trial balance, are shown below.

Journal entries

Account name	Debit £	Credit £
Heat and light		545
Suspense	545	
Rates	786	
Suspense		786
Loan interest expense	269	
Rent received		269

Account name

Account name	Debit £	Credit £
Heat and light	1,200	
Rates	630	
Loan interest expense		104
Rent received	150	

Complete the table below to show the new balances, and whether each will be a debit or a credit.

Account name	Balance £	Debit ✓	Credit ✓
Heat and light			
Rates			
Loan interest expense			
Rent received			

Section 4

ANSWERS TO PRACTICE QUESTIONS

THE BUSINESS ENVIRONMENT

LO1 UNDERSTAND THE PRINCIPLES OF CONTRACT LAW

1   COMMON LAW

B   It is law created by Parliament

D   In the event of conflict with equity the common law will prevail

Law created by Parliament is called statute. In the event of conflict with equity, it will be equity which prevails.

2   CIVIL LAW

	True	False
It is the body of laws that does not relate to criminal offences	✓	
It is law created by judges through decisions made in cases		✓

The law created by judges through decisions in cases is known as case law.

3   CASE LAW I

	True	False
The final court of appeal in the English legal system is the Supreme court	✓	
Obiter dicta is the part of the legal judgement that establishes the precedent that is to be binding on lower courts		✓

The '**ratio decidendi**' is the part of the legal judgement that establishes binding precedent.

4   CASE LAW II

	True	False
Common law developed from local customs	✓	
The Supreme Court can be bound by decisions of the Court of Appeal		✓

5 OFFER AND ACCEPTANCE

C   There is a contract between A and C

A counter-offer was made on the 5th April which brought the offer on the 1st April to an end. There has been no acceptance of this offer. Therefore, there can be no contract between A and B.

6 OFFER AND INVITATION TO TREAT

B   The window display is merely an invitation to treat and the shopkeeper does not have to sell the coat to X.

In **Fisher v Bell** it was established that a window display is an invitation to treat.

7 CONSIDERATION I

	True	False
Consideration must be sufficient	✓	
Past consideration is valid consideration		✓

Past consideration is invalid consideration.

8 CONSIDERATION II

	True	False
Executory consideration is a promise to do something in the future after the contract is made	✓	
Executed consideration is consideration that has been provided in the past		✓

Executed consideration is provided at the time the contract is made.

9 REMEDIES FOR BREACH OF CONTRACT I

	True	False
Damages are a common law remedy.	✓	
Where a judge orders a defendant to perform their contractual obligations this is known as an 'injunction'.		✓

Where a judge orders a defendant to perform their contractual obligations this is known as **'specific performance'**.

10 REMEDIES BREACH OF CONTRACT II

	True	False
A contract contains a term which states a fixed sum is payable in the event of breach. The sum is a genuine pre-estimate of the expected loss. This is an example of a 'penalty clause'.		✓
Adam has a contract with Colin. Four weeks prior to the agreed completion date, Colin telephones Adam out of courtesy to say he has double-booked and will be unable to carry out the work as agreed. This is an example of an 'express anticipatory breach of contract'	✓	

Where the sum is a genuine pre- estimate of the expected loss it is a 'liquidated damages clause' and is enforceable. If the sum is not a genuine pre-estimate it is a 'penalty clause' and is unenforceable.

11 COUNTER-OFFER

A   It destroys the original offer and replaces it with a new offer

12 SHOP WINDOW DISPLAY

A   An invitation to treat

13 REVOCATION OF OFFER

	True	False
Revocation of an offer must be made before the offer is accepted	✓	
Revocation of an offer can be communicated by the offeror or any third party		✓

Revocation of an offer can be made by the offeror or a **reliable** third party.

14 STANDARD OF PROOF

	True	False
The standard of proof required in a civil case is 'on the balance of probabilities	✓	
The standard of proof required in a criminal case is 'beyond any doubt'		✓

The standard of proof required in a criminal case is 'beyond **reasonable** doubt'

15 DELEGATED LEGISLATION

	True	False
Statute and statutory instruments are both forms of delegated legislation		✓
Bye laws and orders in council are both forms of delegated legislation	✓	

Statute (i.e. Acts of Parliament) is primary legislation.

LO2 UNDERSTAND THE EXTERNAL BUSINESS ENVIRONMENT

16 INDIRECT TAXES

    B   Value Added Tax (VAT)

    D   Import duties

17 PERSONAL TAXES

    C   Income tax

    D   Capital gains tax

18 EXCHANGE RATES

Exchange rate movement	Choose from picklist
A movement in the exchange rate results in UK sterling buying fewer Euros than before	UK sterling has depreciated
A movement in the exchange rate results in UK sterling buying more Australian dollars than before	UK sterling has appreciated

19 GOVERNMENT CONTROL

Statement	True / False
An increase in interest rates will lead to an increase in demand for normal goods	False
A reduction in tax rates will lead to an increase in demand for goods and services	True
The annual rate of inflation in a country will always be constant from one year to the next	False

20 TYPES OF TAX

Definition	Type of tax
A tax which takes an increasing proportion of income as income increases	Progressive tax
A tax which takes a fixed proportion of income, irrespective of how high or low that income is	Proportional tax
A tax that takes an increasing proportion of income as it decreases	Regressive tax

21 CHARACTERISTICS OF A GOOD TAX

- Convenient – easy to pay

- Fair – reflect ability to pay

22   FISCAL POLICY

D   Fiscal policy is the use of taxation and government spending to influence the economy

23   INFERIOR GOODS

B   Demand for inferior goods will rise as income falls

24   SUBSTITUTE GOODS

Statement	Choose from picklist
If product A is regarded as a substitute for product B, and the price of product B falls, there will be less demand for product A	True
If products D and E are regarded as substitutes for each other, an increase in the price of product E will result in increase in demand for both products	False

25   COMPLEMENTARY GOODS

B   If the price of product S rises, demand for product T will fall

26   COMPLEMENTARY GOODS II

Statement	✓
A mobile phone	
A safety helmet	✓
A lightweight jacket	
A pair of training shoes	

27   INCOME EFFECT

Statement	✓
If a supplier increases prices, consumers may switch to lower-priced products, leading to a fall in demand	
For expensive items, if a supplier increases prices, consumers may not be able to purchase the product, leading to a fall in demand	✓

28 MICROECONOMICS

Statement	✓
Microeconomics considers aggregate behaviour, producer and consumer behaviour and the workings of the economy as a whole	
Microeconomics considers the economic policies and activities of the government	
Microeconomics considers the economic behaviour and decisions of one industry only	
Microeconomics considers the economic behaviour of individual consumers, firms and industries	✓

29 INCOME TAX

C   A progressive tax

30 BUSINESS TAXES

	Sole trader ✓	Company ✓
Corporation tax		✓
Import duties	✓	✓
Income tax	✓	

LO3 UNDERSTAND KEY PRINCIPLES OF CSR, ETHICS AND SUSTAINABILITY

31 PRINCIPLES

B   Integrity

D   Confidentiality

32 COMPANY SHARES

A   Confidentiality

B   Objectivity

33 TAX ADVICE

D   Professional competence and due care

34 CLIENT DISCUSSION

A   Confidentiality

35   ACCOUNTING LEGISLATION

C   Professional behaviour

D   Professional competence and due care

36   FRAUD

E   Intimidation

37   NEW CLIENT

C   Familiarity

38   3 Ps

C   Profit, People, Planet

39   SUSTAINABLE

E   To look into the possibility of providing the AAT textbook via e-books instead of providing a paper copy to students

40   SUSTAINABILITY

B   Look at installing motion sensor lights into the office block

41   SOLAR PANELS

A   Yes

42   CSR OBJECTIVESS

Practical situation	CSR objective
Your organisation has a policy of encouraging all members of the finance department to study for an appropriate accountancy qualification and proving financial support for those who do so.	Ethical employment practices
Your organisation will shortly introduce 'paperless office' procedures whereby all customer orders are processed online and an accounting software package maintains the sales and purchase ledger accounts.	Environmentally-friendly policies
Your organisation issues a 'Corporate Policy of Ethical Practices' which it requires all potential suppliers to agree to before purchasing goods and services from them	Ethical business practices
Your organisation is currently installing lighting with movement sensors, so that lighting will automatically be switched off if no movement is sensed for 5 minutes. The lighting can be activated by movement only.	Environmentally-friendly policies
Your organisation has a policy, wherever practicable, of permitting employees to work flexible hours, including working from home.	Ethical employment practices

43   BENEFITS

(a)

    B   Use of corporate resources to benefit the community

    C   Employees using voluntary days of absence from work to support charitable activities.

(b)

    B   Greater use of renewable resources to reduce waste

    D   Greater use of recycled materials

44   CORPORATE SOCIAL RESPONSIBILITY

- Encouraging staff travel to work using public transport rather than using their cars

- Installing energy-saving production equipment

- Installing motion sensor lights which turn off when rooms are empty

45   EMPLOYEE WELFARE

- Introducing flexible working conditions for staff

- Offering all staff training and support to those who wish to gain further qualifications

- Providing an on-site gym for all staff to use

LO4 UNDERSTAND THE IMPACT OF SETTING UP DIFFERENT TYPES OF BUSINESS ENTITY

46 THE ENTITY CONCEPT

B   Transactions related to a business must be recorded separately from those of its owners and any other business.

D   While recording transactions in a business we take into account only those events that affect that particular business.

47 BUSINESS ENTITIES

Entity	Description
Sole trader	A business owned and operated by one person
Partnership	A business owned and operated by two or more people
Limited company	A business owned by any number of shareholders

48 TAX IMPLICATIONS

A   Income tax national insurance contributions on the profits

49 OWNERSHIP V MANAGEMENT AND CONTROL

A business does have to be owned and controlled by the same person   – False

A sole trader must work on their own   – False

Owners of a company are the shareholders and are managed by its directors.   – True

A partnership can employ managers to help run the business.   – True

50 LIMITED LIABILITY I

Entity	Limited liability	Unlimited liability
A business owned and operated by one person		✓
A business managed by directors	✓	
A business owned and operated by two or more people		✓

51 LIMITED LIABILITY II

Limited liability means that a business does not have to pay its debts   – False

If a sole trader's business fails their personal assets are protected   – False

A partner is liable for the debts of the partnership if the business fails.   – True

Shareholders are limited in their liability if the company fails.   – True

Directors are personally liable if the company fails   – False

52 LEGAL ADMINISTRATION I

(a)

- Sales and income

- Expenses

- VAT paid and charged (if VAT registered)

- PAYE deducted from employees' salaries

(b)

- Once the submission of the tax return is complete these can be destroyed to save on storage costs   – False

- These records must be kept for five years from the deadline for the submission of the tax return for the period to which they relate.   – True

53 LEGAL ADMINISTRATION II

Description	Documents
The statement confirms that no changes to key information have happened during the year. If changes have been made it states what they are.	**Confirmation statement**
Must be approved and signed on behalf of the board of directors and a copy filed at Companies House.	**Annual financial statements**
These are updated for changes in - members - directors and company secretary - charges - persons with significant control They are kept at the company's registered office and are available for public inspection.	**Statutory registers**
These must show: - details of all money received and spent - a record of assets and liabilities - statement of stocks at end of year. These need to be kept for six years.	**Accounting records**

Picklist: Statutory registers, Profit and loss statement, Accounting records, Confirmation statement, Annual financial statements, Audit

54   BUSINESS FORMATION I

	Sole trader	Partnership	Limited company
There are no legal formalities.	✓	✓	
Must register for corporation tax with HMRC.			✓
They will need to register with HMRC for self-assessment of income tax.	✓		
May have an agreement which sets out matters such as the share of profits		✓	
There is a formal registration process with Companies House with a number of documents that need to be filed:			✓

55   BUSINESS FORMATION II

D   A partnership must have a partnership agreement

56   PRE-INCORPORATION CONTRACTS I

B   The company is bound by the contract.

57   BUSINESS FORMATION III

Once a company has been formed it is known as '**incorporated**'

58   COMPANIES HOUSE REGISTRATION

Document	Required	Not required
Memorandum of association	✓	
Business plans		✓
Application for registration	✓	
Statement of capital	✓	
Statement of consent to act	✓	
Statement of creditworthiness		✓
Statement of compliance	✓	

59   PRE-INCORPORATION CONTRACTS II

B   By and against the accountant only

60   OFF THE SHELF COMPANY

- May have unsettled liabilities
- Some documents will need to be submitted to Companies House which will need to be tailored to the company.

LO5 UNDERSTAND THE FINANCE FUNCTION WITHIN AN ORGANISATION

61   POLICIES AND PROCEDURES

  A   Data Protection Act

  B   Health and Safety at Work

  D   Authorised Signatory Procedure

62   DOCUMENTS

Department	Document	
Purchasing Department	(b)	Copy of Purchase order
HR Department	(d)	New employee forms
Payroll Department	(e)	Statutory Sick pay forms

63   DEPARTMENTS

Department	Information
Sales Dept.	Commission payable to sales staff
Accounts Dept.	Bank statements
Payroll Dept.	List of all new employees for the period

64   SERVICE PROVISION

  • Budget report analysis

  • Payment of sales commission

65   STAKEHOLDERS

  • HM Revenue & Customs

  • Receivables

66   REPORTING LINES

Person	Should report to the following
Sales and Purchase Ledger Assistant	Accounts department manager
Administration Assistant	General manager
3 Sales Assistants	Sales manager
Payroll Assistant	Accounts department manager
Accounting Department Manager	Finance director

67 PERSON AND ROLE

Role	Reports to
Accounts assistant	Accounting department manager
Sales Ledger clerk	Accounting department manager
Machine operator	Factory manager

68 COMPLIANCE AND SOLVENCY

Action	Legal Compliance	Solvency
Ensure financial statements are filed on time	✓	
Improve credit control procedures		✓
Maintain a petty cash book		
Create and maintain a cash budget		✓
Ensure the work place is a safe environment for staff and visitors	✓	

69 THE FINANCE FUNCTION

Actions	Efficient running of the business	Solvency of the business	Legal Compliance
Monitor cash flow		✓	
Provide quotation to customer			
Ensure Sales Tax is paid to HMRC on time			✓
Regularly chase outstanding receivables		✓	
Ensure inventory is ordered when it falls to the minimum level	✓		
Ensure members of staff are first aid trained			✓
Regular maintenance of machinery	✓		
Produce a staff rota for tea making			

70 ISSUES

- The paper for the photocopier keeps running out without a new order being placed.
- Somebody in the office continues to prop the fire door open.

71 PETTY CASH

- Fraudulent activity may have taken place and go undetected

72 CONFLICT

Issue	Resolve myself	Refer to line manager
Your manager has asked you to complete a Statement of Financial position, however you do not have the accounting knowledge to do this		✓
You suspect your colleague knows your computer password	✓	
You suspect an expenses form which has been passed to you has non-business expenses on it and the form has been submitted by a manager		✓

73 OUTSOURCING

- How costly will the use of the service company be relative to hiring a new payroll clerk?

- How easy will it be to find a payroll clerk with the appropriate skills and experience?

- Will the payroll services company be able to provide additional services beyond what could be produced in-house e.g. detailed analytical information about overtime worked?

- Does the service company have a good reputation for quality and reliability?

- What security measures does the service company have in place to protect our employees' data?

74 COMMUNICATION

Activity	Description
Encoding	The sender deciding what information needs to be communicated.
Transmitting	The means of communication used.
Decoding	The recipient receiving and understanding the message.
Feedback	The response to the message. It may be a simple acknowledgement of receipt and that the message is understood or a request for clarification or additional information.
Noise/interference	Anything that undermines or prevents the successful transmission of a message.

75 OVERDRAFT

Based on the summary provided the FD should ensure a facility of £4,000 is available by the end of August.

However, given the uncertainty associated with forecasts and the small positive bank balances shown in July and August it will be sensible to seek a larger facility by the end of June.

LO6 PRODUCE WORK IN APPROPRIATE FORMATS AND COMMUNICATE EFFECTIVELY

76   MRS MAY

Dear Mrs May,

Invoice 3576 – 10 units of ZXY

I have recently checked the details of your invoice 3576 relating to the purchase of 10 units of product ZXY. The unit price stated on the invoice of £63 is incorrect; it should be £36.

Please issue a credit note to cancel your invoice 3576 and issue a new invoice using the correct unit price of £36. When we have received the credit note and corrected invoice, I will arrange to make payment to you.

Yours sincerely

Financial Assistant

77   BILLY

Dear Billy,

I was very cheesed to here that you did not receive your goods in proper working order. We have very strict internal procedures, which are designed to prevent faulty goods reaching our customers. Please be assured that we are investigating fully you're case and are striving to ensure that this does not happen again in the future.

By way of an apolojy we will be refunding you in full and offering you a 20% discount on your next purchase.

Kind regards

John Anderson

Store manager

78   MR CADBURY

Dear Mr Cadbury

I enclose a copy of the invoice which **your** requested during **are** telephone conversation this morning.

Please note this invoice is dated **31** June and **therefor** is overdue for payment.

I look forward to receiving your cheque in full settlement by return of post.

Yours **faithfully**

79   BOB

From: bob@accountancyfirm.co.uk

To: ally@accountancyfirm.co.uk

Subject: AAT Exam Performance

Hello Ally,

I would like to discuss the above with you tomorrow afternoon. In particular I would like to review the performance of John Barnes with a view to finding out why he has performed poorly. I also hope we can resolve this issue by working together with John.

Regards

Bob

80   K KIPLING

From AATstudent@Kaplan.co.uk

To: kk@cakes4tea.org.uk

Subject: Meeting confirmation – Mrs Anna Howes

Good morning Mr Kipling

Following our telephone conversation I confirm the meeting which is to take place at your premises on Monday at 2.30pm.

I will bring a copy of the business plan I have prepared.

Kind regards

Anna Howes

81   JOSHUA VALENTINE

From: AATstudent@atoz.org.uk

To: jvalentine@atoz.org.uk; cjenton@atoz.org.uk; dwheeler@atoz.org.uk

Subject: Conference

Hello All,

This conference is being held at King's Hotel on Thursday at 10 am.

The conference will be held regarding the issue of recycling within organisations.

Please confirm your attendance.

Regards,

AAT Student

82   PURCHASE OF LAPTOPS

To: j.wriggle@kplittle.co.uk

From: b.coalie@kplittle.co.uk

Subject: Laptops

Date: 2 October 20X8

Hi Joe,

I'm pleased to inform you that we have been able to approve your purchase request for 6 laptops. The budget has been set at £6,000 in total for all 6 laptops.

You will need to speak with the relevant sales team staff so that they are aware their laptop will be replaced in the near future.

If you have any further questions, please do not hesitate to contact me.

Kind regards,

Bernie

83   REPORT CONTENT

	Introduction	Appendices
Information regarding what the report is based upon	✓	
Supporting calculations for figures contained within the body of the report		✓

84

A memo	
A business report	
An e-mail	✓
A mobile phone text message	

85

An outline of the company and what it does	✓
The full financial statements of the company	
A business report analysing other companies providing wedding services	
Her personal CV, including her education and past work experience	

86

Hi Steven	
Hello	
Dear Mr Crowfoot	✓
Dear Badger	

87

Thanks for everything, Claire	
Best wishes, Claire	
Yours faithfully, Claire	
Yours sincerely, Claire	✓

88

See you later, Claire	
Kind regards, Claire	✓
Yours faithfully, Claire	
Yours sincerely, Claire	

89   D   The actual cost of production of the muffins

90   A   A memo

LO7 UNDERSTAND THE IMPORTANCE OF INFORMATION TO BUSINESS OPERATIONS

91 INFORMATION

(a)

- understandable
- relevant and reliable
- consistent
- timely
- comparable

(b)

- Only information stated in monetary terms is useful to accountants – False
- Non-financial information is useful information to individuals who make decisions – True

92 NEW CUSTOMER

	Characteristic
Sarah	Timely
Amit	Relevant and reliable

93 PEPPER & MINT

Advantages

- It is easier to collect useful data about specific customers and their purchase history in order to better target advertising and promotions.
- The company will have better data with which to understand its customer base e.g. gender, age groups, value per transaction etc.
- Customers will not have to input their data every time they purchase making subsequent purchases quicker and improving data security.

Disadvantages

- Customers may be sensitive about their data and not wish to set-up an account.
- Customers may buy from competitors who do offer a 'guest' option as they consider it to be easier than setting up an account.
- More detailed information will be held by the company about its customers increasing the risks and costs associated with data protection compliance and security.

94   INVENTORY

- Goods received note

The goods received note is raised by goods inwards only when the goods are received and accepted into inventory.

95   FIRE!

- Regular electrical safety testing
- A fire suppression system designed not to damage electronics
- Use of cloud accounting software
- Daily back-ups of data stored off-site or in a fire-proof safe

96   PASSWORD

- There is a lack of segregation as Francisco's password allows him wide access to the accounting system when he should only have access to the payables ledger.
- Simple passwords like 'QWERTY' should be avoided as they can be guessed.
- Passwords should be regularly changed.
- A password should never be written down as if found, will allow access to unauthorised users.
- A password should not be shared with colleagues.

97   REVENUE

The large amount recognised on a Sunday is unexpected because sales only occur Monday to Friday. Furthermore, transactions processed outside of normal hours can be an indicator of fraud.

98   RECEIPTS

- Remittance advice

99   BUDGETARY INFORMATION

- To assist managers in decision making and control.

100   CLOUD

- Data can be accessed at any time, from any location, on a variety of devices.
- The accounting information is updated in real-time.
- The data is automatically backed-up by the cloud accounting service provider.

101 VIRUSES

- Use anti-virus software to prevent corruption of the system by viruses.

- Anti-virus software must be kept up-to-date.

- Approval of external software by the IT department.

- Use of only tested, marked disks/memory sticks.

- Restricted access to CDs & flash drives on all PCs/workstations.

- Strong password controls.

102 DEPARTMENTS I

Information supplied	Sales and distribution	Warehouse
Revenue broken down by customer	✓	
Inventory holding period by inventory line		✓
Advertising expenditure by product range	✓	

103 DEPARTMENTS II

Information supplied	Production	Payroll
National insurance rates		✓
Raw materials cost per unit	✓	
Employee PAYE codes		✓

104 TECHNOLOGY

Statement	True	False
Pre-set passwords set by the manufacturer must be changed to individually selected, unique passwords as soon as possible.	✓	
The purpose of air-conditioning in the computer environment is solely for the comfort of those working in that environment.		✓

Pre-set passwords are less secure.

The primary purpose of air-conditioning in the computer environment is to stop computers over-heating which causes a reduction in performance. When computers over-heat the speed of the processor is reduced in order to reduce the output of heat– this is known a 'thermal-throttling'.

105 GOAL SETTING

- Inventory movement records
- Sales records by inventory line

Section 5

ANSWERS TO PRACTICE QUESTIONS

ITBK L01 UNDERSTAND HOW TO SET UP BOOKKEEPING SYSTEMS

106   LEO LTD

(a)

General ledger code	GL530
Customer account code	DEF14

(b)

To help trace orders and amounts due from particular customers

107   ELLA'S PAINTS

(a)

General ledger code	GL395
Supplier account code	MEG20

(b)

To help trace orders and amounts due to particular suppliers

108   ROBERTO & CO

(a)

Supplier account code	ALE1
General ledger code	GL72

(b)

To help calculate expense incurred in a GL account

109 ACCOUNTING EQUATION 1

(a)

Item	True/False
Assets less capital is equal to liabilities	True
Assets plus liabilities are equal to capital	False
Capital plus liabilities are equal to assets	True

(b)

Item	Asset or liability?
Inventory	Asset
Machinery	Asset
5 year loan	Liability

110 CLASSIFICATION

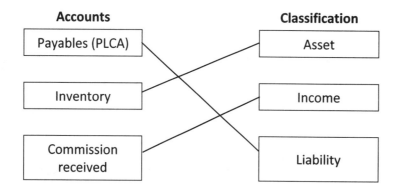

111 ACCOUNTING EQUATION 2

(a)

Item	True/False
Capital is equal to assets plus liabilities	False
Assets less liabilities are equal to capital	True
Liabilities are equal to capital plus assets	False

(b)

Item	Asset or liability?
VAT owed to tax authorities	Liability
Amounts owing to payables	Liability
Money in the bank	Asset

112 CAPEX

Item	Capital income	Revenue income	Capital expenditure	Revenue expenditure
Receipt from sale of motor vehicle	✓			
Receipts from credit sales		✓		
Purchase of machinery			✓	
Payment of electricity bill				✓
Purchase of goods for resale				✓

113 REVEX

Item	Capital income	Revenue income	Capital expenditure	Revenue expenditure
Receipt from sale of machinery	✓			
Payment of telephone bill				✓
Purchase of building			✓	
Receipts from cash sales		✓		
Receipts from receivables		✓		

114 EXPENDITURE TYPES

Item	Capital expenditure	Revenue expenditure	Capital income	Revenue income
Purchase of a new computer system	✓			
Receipts from customers				✓
Receipt from sale of fixtures and fittings			✓	
Payments of salaries to staff		✓		
Purchase of cleaning materials		✓		
Receipt of bank interest				✓

115 ASSET OR LIABILITY

(a)

Item	Asset or liability?
Factory building	Asset
Money due to suppliers	Liability
Car used in the business	Asset

(b)　The expense electricity will **increase**; the asset of bank will **decrease**.

116 ACCOUNTING EQUATION 3

Assets £	Liabilities £	Capital £
158,360	28,870	129,490

117 MULTIPLE CHOICE 1

(a)

		Capital expenditure or revenue expense
(i)	Work to install additional, high-specification, electrical power cabling and circuits so that additional plant and equipment can become operational	Capital
(ii)	Replacement of some loose and damaged roof tiles following a recent storm	Revenue
(iii)	Repainting the factory administration office	Revenue
(iv)	Modifications to the factory entrance to enable a large item of plant and equipment to be installed	Capital

(b)　**C**　It is a summary of assets, liabilities and equity at a specified date

(c)　**Debit balances:**　　　　　　　　　　**Credit balances:**

　　C　Assets and expenses　　　　Liabilities, capital and revenues

118 MULTIPLE CHOICE 2

(a)　**D**　It is a summary of income and expenditure for an accounting period

(b)　**D**　Assets and expenses normally have debit balances

(c)　**B**　A debit balance exists where the total of debit entries is less than the total of credit entries

119 LEO

(a)

	TRANSACTION	CASH	CREDIT
(i)	Receipt of goods worth £140.59 from a supplier together with an invoice for that amount.		✓
(ii)	Payment of £278.50 by cheque for a purchase at the till.	✓	
(iii)	Receipt of a deposit of £15.00 for goods.	✓	
(iv)	Sending of an invoice for £135.00 to the payer of the deposit for the remaining value of the goods.		✓
(v)	Sale of goods for £14.83, payment received by credit card.	✓	

(b)
(i)   Asset – inventory

(ii)   Expense

(iii)   Income

(iv)   Asset – trade receivables

(v)   Expense

(vi)   Liability (this is a special liability known as capital)

(vii)   Liability – payables

(viii)   Asset

(ix)   Asset

(x)   Income

(xi)   Asset

120 ACCOUNT CODES

(a)

Date	Customer name	Customer account code
1 August	Worthington Ltd	CWORT092
4 August	Moss Plc	CMOSS093

Date	Supplier name	Supplier account code
2 August	Morley & Sons	SMORL076
5 August	Chapman Ltd	SCHAP077

(b)

Statement	True ✓	False ✓
The reconciliation between the individual payables ledger and the control account is completed automatically	✓	
General ledger accounts need to be manually balanced off to extract a trial balance		✓

(c)

Consequence	✓
The total sales value will be understated	✓
The business may despatch goods that have not been sold	
The total amount owed to payables will be understated	
The business may be paid for goods that have not been sold	
The business may pay the incorrect amount to a supplier	
The business will receive more money from a customer than they are expecting per their customer report	✓

Feedback:

Item 1: Sales would have been debited rather than credited resulting in understatement. Item 2: Goods are despatched on generation of a sales order, not an invoice or credit note. Item 3: Errors over sales affects receivables rather than payables. Item 4: The business should be paid the right amount as a sales invoice was correctly sent to the customer. Item 5: The transaction invoices sales rather than purchases. Item 6: The business will have understated receivables and as a result will be paid more than they expect.

(d)

Summarising the transactions for a period and classifying them into relevant categories of income and expenditure to show the overall profit or loss for the period	Statement of profit or loss
Detailing all of the transactions with a credit customer during the period and advising a credit customer of the balance outstanding on their account	Supplier statement
To summarise the balances on each of the general ledger accounts in order to begin the preparation of the financial statements	Trial balance
To correct an invoice that has been prepared incorrectly by overstating the value of goods supplied	Credit note

121 PRINCIPLES 1

(a)

Assets £	Liabilities £	Capital £
£21,236.90	£9,929.45	£11,307.45

Feedback:

Assets = £10,180.00 + £4,367.45 + £2,100.00 + £4,589.45 = £21,236.90

Liabilities = £8,392.48 + £1,536.97 = £9,929.45

Capital = Assets – Liabilities = £21,236.90 – £9,929.45 = £11,307.45

(b)

Transaction 1	
Effect	✓
Increase assets	✓
Decrease assets	
Increase capital	
Increase liabilities	✓
Decrease liabilities	

Transaction 2	
Effect	✓
Increase liabilities	
Increase capital	✓
Decrease capital	
Increase assets	✓
Decrease liabilities	

Feedback:

Transaction 1 – Dr Non-current assets, Cr Payables

Transaction 2 – Dr Cash, Cr Inventory, Cr Capital

Note: the increase in cash will exceed the reduction in inventory as the goods were sold at a profit.

(c)

Account balance	Debit ✓	Credit ✓
Opening inventory	✓	
Payables		✓
Drawings	✓	

122 DIGITAL BOOKKEEPING

(a)

Details	Ledger code		Details	Ledger code
Sales – dog food	2019		Insurance expense	3072
Sales – dog bedding	2020		Courier expense	3073
Sales – dog toys	2021		Advertising expense	3074

Feedback: As these are new general ledger codes, we can assume they will run in sequence from the first ones given in the question.

(b)

Coding system	✓
Alphanumerical	
Alphabetical	
Numerical	✓

Feedback: only numbers are used in the coding system.

(c)

Consequence	✓
Assets will be understated	✓
Sales will be understated	
Purchases will be understated	
Expenses will be overstated	✓

(d)

Statement	True ✓	False ✓
It is not possible to post a duplicate transaction using a digital bookkeeping system		✓
Digital bookkeeping systems can automatically post recurring entries	✓	
The trial balance will automatically balance using a digital bookkeeping system	✓	

Feedback:

Item 1 – the operator could post the same transaction into the system twice. Item 2 – this is a typical function of digital systems. Item 3 – Digital systems will always process matching debits and credits although may use a suspense account.

123 PRINCIPLES 2

(a)

Item	
Motor vehicles	Assets
Insurance costs	Expenses
Drawings	Capital
Payables	Liabilities

(b)

Transaction	Dual effect 1	Dual effect 2
Owner invests £20,000 cash into the business bank account	Increases assets	Increases capital
Purchases a laptop computer for use within the business, paying in cash	Increases assets	Decreases assets
Makes a sale to a customer realising a profit on the sale. Customer agrees to pay at a later date	Increases capital	Increases assets
Owner withdraws £10,000 cash from the business to pay for a private holiday	Decreases assets	Decreases capital
A credit customer pays the amount owed	Increases assets	Decreases assets

Feedback: Item 1 – This is capital introduced. Item 2 – Non-current assets increase, but cash reduces by an equivalent amount. Item 3 – Trade receivables increase by more than the reduction in inventory (as a profit has been made). Item 4 – Cash decreases and the drawings also result in a decrease in capital. Item 5 – Cash increases and trade receivables decrease by an equivalent amount.

(c)

£	3,300.00

Feedback: Assets – liabilities = Capital

Office equipment + £4,593.90 + £1,342.80 + £1030.00 – £6,780.00 = £3,486.70

Rearrange the equation:

Office equipment = £3,486.70 – £4,593.90 – £1,342.80 – £1030.00 + £6,780.00 = £3,300.00

124 PRINCIPLES 3

(a)

Item	Capital expenditure	Revenue expenditure	Capital income	Revenue income
Purchase of computer equipment	✓			
Receipts from credit sales				✓
Receipt from sale of motor vehicle (non-current asset)			✓	
Purchase of motor vehicle	✓			
Purchase of stationery		✓		
Payment of rent		✓		

(b)

Statement	True ✓	False ✓
Assets less liabilities are equal to capital	✓	
The business and owner are treated as two separate entities	✓	
A debit increases an item of income		✓

(c)

Item	Option
Computer equipment	Assets
Petty cash	Assets
Money owed to suppliers	Liabilities

ITBK L02 PROCESS CUSTOMER TRANSACTIONS

125 ALESSANDRO LTD

(a)

	**Alessandro Ltd** **8 Alan Street** **Glasgow, G1 7DJ** **VAT Registration No. 398 2774 01**

Palermo Wholesale
167 Front St
Stanley
DH8 4TJ

Customer account code: AGG42

Delivery note number: 24369
Date: 1 Aug 20XX

Invoice No: 327

Quantity	Product code	Total list price £	Net amount after discount £	VAT £	Gross £
40	SB05	2,500	2,200	440	2,640

(b)

Prompt payment discount

126 HLB WHOLESALE

(a)

Painting Supplies Ltd
19 Edmund St
Newcastle, NE6 5DJ

VAT Registration No. 402 2958 02

HLB Wholesale
98 Back St
Consett
DH4 3PD

Date: 1 Feb 20XX

Customer account code: HLB24

Delivery note number: 46589

Invoice No: 298

Quantity	Product code	Total list price £	Net amount after discount £	VAT £	Gross £
20	SD19	300	270	54	324

(b)

Trade discount

127 MASHED LTD

(a)

Hickory House
22 Nursery Road
Keighley, BD22 7BD

VAT Registration No. 476 1397 02

Mashed Ltd
42 Moorside Court
Ilkley
Leeds, LS29 4PR

Customer account code: MA87

Delivery note number: 472

Date: 1 Aug 20XX

Invoice No: 47

Quantity of pots	Product code	Total list price £	Net amount after discount £	VAT £	Gross £
20	P10	100	90	18	108

(b)

Bulk discount

128 ROCKY RICARDO

(a)

Rocky Ricardo
1 Rocky Way
Middleton, M42 5TU

VAT Registration No. 298 3827 04

Alpha Group
Alpha House
Warwick
WR11 5TB

Customer account code: ALP01

Delivery note number: 2132

Date: 1 Dec 20XX

Invoice No: 950

Quantity of cases	Product code	Total list price £	Net amount after discount £	VAT £	Gross £
200	A1	2,000	1,800	360	2,160

(b)

Sales daybook					
Date 20XX	Details	Invoice No:	Total £	VAT £	Net £
1 Dec	Alpha Group	950	2,160	360	1,800

(c)

Invoice 189

(d) **(i)**

£594

(ii)

£600

129 SDB

Sales daybook

Date 20XX	Details	Invoice number	Total £	VAT £	Net £	Sales type 1 £	Sales type 2 £
31 Dec	Poonams	105	3,600	600	3,000		3,000
31 Dec	D. Taylor	106	7,680	1,280	6,400	6,400	
31 Dec	Smiths	107	3,840	640	3,200		3,200
	Totals		15,120	2,520	12,600	6,400	6,200

130 MAHINDRA LTD

Sales daybook

Date 20XX	Details	Invoice number	Total £	VAT £	Net £	Sales type 1 £	Sales type 2 £
31 Jan	Square Ltd	3567	1,200	200	1,000	1,000	
31 Jan	Oval & Co	3568	9,600	1,600	8,000		8,000
31 Jan	Diamond Ltd	3569	13,200	2,200	11,000		11,000
31 Jan	Triangle Ltd	3570	7,920	1,320	6,600	6,600	
	Totals		31,920	5,320	26,600	7,600	19,000

131 PAR FOR THE COURSE GOLF SUPPLIES

(a)

Discount type	✓
Prompt payment	
Trade	
Bulk	✓

Feedback: Remember that bulk discount relates to discount given by a supplier for sales orders above a certain quantity.

(b)

	£
Net amount after discounts	2,685.00
VAT @ 20%	537.00
Total	3,222.00

Feedback: Net amount = (300 × £5) + (150 × £7.90) = £2,685

(c)

Menu option	✓
Purchases daybook	
Purchase returns daybook	
Cash book	
Sales daybook	✓
Sales returns daybook	
Discounts allowed daybook	
Discounts received daybook	

Date	Customer code	Customer	General ledger code	Invoice number	Net £	VAT code
13 Aug	EREH094	Erehwon Golf Club	Option 1	2808	2,685.00	Option 2

Option 1	✓
1001 Sales – golf equipment	✓
1002 Sales – golf buggies	
4001 Purchases – golf equipment	
7001 Receivables	

Option 2	✓
V0 – 0%	
V5 – 5%	
V20 – 20%	✓

132   LINKEES TOY MAKERS LTD

(a)

Discount type	✓
Prompt payment	✓
Trade	
Bulk	

(b)

	£
Net amount after discounts	675.00
VAT @ 20%	135.00
Total	810.00

(c)

Menu option	✓
Purchases daybook	
Purchase returns daybook	
Cash book	
Sales daybook	✓
Sales returns daybook	
Discounts allowed daybook	
Discounts received daybook	

Date	Customer code	Customer	General ledger code	Invoice number	Net £	VAT code
17 May	THOM08	Thomas' Toys	Option 1	2808	675.00	Option 2

Option 1	✓
1001 Sales – toys	
1002 Sales – board games	✓
4001 Purchases – Inventory	
7001 Receivables	

Option 2	✓
V0 – 0%	
V5 – 5%	
V20 – 20%	✓
V1 – Exempt	

133 WILLIAM & SAMMY LTD

(a)

Sales invoice 286

(b)

£4,481.28

(c)

£4,668.00

134 DIAMONDS & RUBIES LTD

<table>
<tr><td colspan="4" align="center">Stavros
121 Baker St
Newcastle, NE1 7DJ</td></tr>
<tr><td colspan="2">To: Diamonds & Rubies Ltd</td><td colspan="2">Date: 31 Aug 20XX</td></tr>
<tr><td>Date
20XX</td><td>Details</td><td align="center">Transaction amount
£</td><td align="center">Outstanding amount
£</td></tr>
<tr><td>5 Aug</td><td>Invoice 3927</td><td align="center">4,640</td><td align="center">4,640</td></tr>
<tr><td>10 Aug</td><td>Credit note 96</td><td align="center">980</td><td align="center">3,660</td></tr>
<tr><td>21 Aug</td><td>Invoice 3964</td><td align="center">1,560</td><td align="center">5,220</td></tr>
<tr><td>28 Aug</td><td>Credit note 104</td><td align="center">650</td><td align="center">4,570</td></tr>
<tr><td>30 Aug</td><td>Cheque received</td><td align="center">2,100</td><td align="center">2,470</td></tr>
</table>

135 MAX LTD

<table>
<tr><td colspan="4" align="center">Painting Supplies Ltd
19 Edmund St
Newcastle, NE6 5DJ</td></tr>
<tr><td colspan="2">To: Max Ltd</td><td colspan="2">Date: 28 Feb 20XX</td></tr>
<tr><td>Date
20XX</td><td>Details</td><td align="center">Transaction amount
£</td><td align="center">Outstanding amount
£</td></tr>
<tr><td>5 Feb</td><td>Invoice 4658</td><td align="center">2,560</td><td align="center">2,560</td></tr>
<tr><td>11 Feb</td><td>Invoice 3964</td><td align="center">3,290</td><td align="center">5,850</td></tr>
<tr><td>21 Feb</td><td>Credit note 125</td><td align="center">230</td><td align="center">5,620</td></tr>
<tr><td>23 Feb</td><td>Credit note 139</td><td align="center">560</td><td align="center">5,060</td></tr>
<tr><td>27 Feb</td><td>Cheque received</td><td align="center">1,900</td><td align="center">3,160</td></tr>
</table>

136   BETA BOARDS

	Beta Boards		
	3 Victoria Avenue		
	Troon		
	KA5 2BD		
To: Ava Ltd		**Date:** 31 Aug 20XX	
Date 20XX	**Details**	**Transaction amount £**	**Outstanding amount £**
10 Aug	Invoice 222	350	350
12 Aug	Cheque	225	125
15 Aug	Invoice 305	744	869
20 Aug	Credit note 194	339	530
24 Aug	Cheque	530	0

137   BELLA PUMPKIN

(a) – (b)

Bella Pumpkin

Date 20XX	Details	Amount £	Date 20XX	Details	Amount £
12 Dec	Invoice 1001	1,700	21 Dec	Credit note 101	940
21 Dec	Invoice 1004	2,350	29 Dec	Cheque rec'd	2,000
27 Dec	Invoice 1010	470	31 Dec	Balance c/d	1,580
		4,520			**4,520**
20XY 1 Jan	Balance b/d	1,580			

(c)

	Rocky Ricardo		
	1 Rocky Way		
	Middleton, M42 5TU		
To: Bella Pumpkin		**Date:** 31 Dec 20XX	
Date 20XX	**Details**	**Transaction amount £**	**Outstanding amount £**
12 Dec	Invoice 1001	1,700	1,700
21 Dec	Invoice 1004	2,350	4,050
21 Dec	Credit note 101	940	3,110
27 Dec	Invoice 1010	470	3,580
29 Dec	Cheque	2,000	1,580

138 LAYLA LTD

(a)

Transaction type	Date	Details	Amount £	Action
Balance b/f	1 Aug 20XX		473.87	Allocate full amount – 3671
Invoice 1046	4 Aug 20XX	Goods	1,059.60	Query underpayment
Invoice 1059	9 Aug 20XX	Services	462.20	Query overpayment
Invoice 1068	10 Aug 20XX	Goods	789.48	Allocate full amount – 3684
Invoice 1096	14 Aug 20XX	Goods	662.20	Allocate full amount – 3684

Feedback:

Balance b/f – This amount matches the amount remitted against Invoice 1028. Action is to allocate full amount – in relation to remittance 3671.

Invoice 1046 – The amount remitted of £1,006.62 is £1,059.60 less 5% settlement discount. However, the invoice was settled 12 days after it was raised so the discount should not have been taken. Action is to query underpayment.

Invoice 1059 – The amount remitted of £462.20 is equivalent to the amount of the invoice. However, this was paid within 7 days so qualifies for the settlement discount. Action is to query overpayment.

Invoice 1068 – The amount remitted of £789.48 is equivalent to the amount of the invoice which does not qualify for a settlement discount as paid after 12 days. Action is to allocate full amount – in relation to remittance 3684.

Invoice 1096 – The amount remitted of £629.09 is equivalent to the amount of the invoice less settlement discount which it qualifies for as paid within 10 days of the invoice date. Action is to allocate full amount – in relation to remittance 3684.

(b)

Customer name	Invoice number	Amount before discount £	Amount after prompt payment discount £
Oliver John & Co	387	8,345.60	7,928.32
Excelsior Ltd	395	4,562.40	4,334.28

(c)

Customer name	Prompt payment Discount %	Invoice amount £	Amount paid £	Amount that should have been paid £	Amount outstanding £
Galahad	5	7,529.40	7,093.52	7,152.93	59.41

Feedback: The correct payment is £7,529.40 × 95% = £7,152.93

139   KLOPP & CO

(a)

Transaction type	Date	Details	Amount £	Action
Balance b/f	1 Apr 20XX		752.34	Allocate full amount – 2976
Invoice 354	2 Apr 20XX	Goods	475.61	Allocate full amount – 2976
Invoice 362	9 Apr 20XX	Services	834.25	Query underpayment
Invoice 371	12 Apr 20XX	Services	245.50	Allocate full amount – 2976
Invoice 379	13 Apr 20XX	Goods	1,051.34	Allocate full amount – 3018
Credit note 46	14 Apr 20XX	Correction – 379	178.72	Allocate full amount – 3018
Invoice 383	14 Apr 20XX	Goods	649.23	Allocate full amount – 3018
Invoice 391	19 Apr 20XX	Goods	507.75	Allocate full amount – 3018

Feedback:

Invoice 342 – the invoice made up the opening balance of £752.34. The opening balance is dated 1 April so does not qualify for a settlement discount as the remittance is dated 17 April which is more than the required discount period of 7 days. The full balance of £752.34 has been received. Action is to allocate the full amount – in relation to remittance 2976.

Invoice 354 – the invoice amount is £475.61. The invoice date is 2 April so does not qualify for a settlement discount as the remittance is dated 17 April which is more than the required period of 7 days. The full balance of £475.61 has been received. Action is to allocate the full amount – in relation to remittance 2976.

Invoice 362 – the invoice amount is £834.25 and the invoice is dated 9 April so does not qualify for a settlement discount as the remittance is dated 17 April which is more than the required period of 7 days. The amount received is £800.88 (the settlement discount has been incorrectly deducted). Action is to query the underpayment.

Invoice 371 – the invoice amount is £245.50 and the invoice is dated 12 April so qualifies for a settlement discount as the remittance is dated 17 April which is less than the required period of 7 days. The discounted amount of £235.68 (£245.50 × 96%) has been correctly received. Action is to allocate the full amount – in relation to remittance 2976.

Invoice 379 and Credit Note 46 – The invoice did not qualify for a prompt payment discount. The invoice amount of £1,051.34 less the credit note amount of £178.72 equates to £872.62 which agrees to what was remitted. Action is to allocate the full amount – in relation to remittance 3018.

Invoice 383 – the invoice amount is £649.23 and the invoice is dated 14 April so does not qualify for a settlement discount as the remittance is dated 24 April which is more than the required period of 7 days. The amount of £649.23 has been correctly received. Action is to allocate the full amount – in relation to remittance 3018.

Invoice 391 – the invoice amount is £507.75 and the invoice is dated 19 April so qualifies for a settlement discount as the remittance is dated 24 April which is less than the required period of 7 days. The discounted amount of £487.44 (£507.75 × 96%) has been correctly received. Action is to allocate the full amount – in relation to remittance 3018.

(b)

Reason	✓
The customer has taken a prompt payment discount of 6% that they were not entitled to, on an invoice of £1,958 before the discount.	✓
Henderson & Co have duplicated an invoice in their system for £96.90 plus 20% VAT.	
2 credit notes for £49.71 and £67.77 have been omitted by Henderson & Co.	✓
The customer has paid for £117.48 of goods that they never received.	

Feedback: Item 1 – results in an underpayment of £1,958 × 6% = £117.48. Item 2 – the duplicated invoice amounts to a gross amount of £96.90 × 120% = £116.28. Item 3 – The credit notes amount to £117.48 resulting in a payment less than expected. Item 4 – If the customer paid for goods not received it would result in an overpayment.

ITBK L03 PROCESS SUPPLIER TRANSACTIONS

140 NAN NURSING

(a) Has the correct purchase price of the chocolate puddings been charged on the invoice?

N

(b) Has the correct discount been applied?

Y

(c) What would be the VAT amount charged if the invoice was correct?

£18.00

(d) What would be the total amount charged if the invoice was correct?

£108.00

141 PIXIE PAPER

(a) Has the correct product been supplied by Pixie Paper?

Y

(b) Has the correct net price been calculated?

N

(c) Has the total invoice price been calculated correctly?

N

(d) What would be the VAT amount charged if the invoice was correct?

£90.00

(e) What would be the total amount charged if the invoice was correct?

£540.00

Feedback re (b) – the trade discount of 10% should have been deducted so that the net price was £450. VAT @ 20% on the net price of £450 is then calculated as £90.00.

142 PAINTS R US

   (a) Has the correct product been supplied?   Y

   (b) Has the correct net price been calculated?   Y

   (c) Has the total invoice price been calculated correctly?   N

   (d) What would be the VAT amount charged if the invoice was correct?   £32.00

   (e) What would be the total amount charged if the invoice was correct?   £192.00

143 MT MOTORS

   (a) **B** £400.00

	£
List price	500
Less: Trade discount (20% × £500)	(100)
Purchases	400

   (b) **B** £80.00

	£
List price	500.00
Less: Trade discount	(100.00)
Net purchases	400.00
VAT @ 20%	80.00
	480.00

   (c) **A** It is issued to a supplier to request supply of goods from them on terms specified within the order.

144 ECHO LTD

   (a)

     Has the correct discount been applied?   N

     How much should the trade discount amount be?   £100

     What would be the VAT amount charged if the invoice was correct?   £180

   (b)

Daybook: Purchase daybook					
Date 20XX	Details	Invoice No:	Total £	VAT £	Net £
10 Dec	Messi Brothers	1365	2,250	375	1,875

145 GORDON'S TRAIN REPAIRS

(a)

Daybook	✓
Sales daybook	
Purchases daybook	
Cashbook	
Purchase returns daybook	✓
Sales returns daybook	
Discounts allowed daybook	

(b)

Date 20XX	Supplier	Credit note number	Net £	VAT £	Total £
17 May	Narrow Gauge Ltd	CN869	317.60	63.52	381.12
26 June	Island of Sodor plc	CN0289	84.00	16.80	100.80
8 Aug	Topham Hatt & Co	421	98.50	19.70	118.20
13 Sep	Flying Kipper Ltd	C980	206.00	41.20	247.20
14 Oct	Gordon's Train Repairs	CN483	476.50	95.30	571.80
		Totals	1,182.60	236.52	1,419.12

(c)

Discrepancy	✓
Date of invoice	
Product type	
Quantity of product	
Unit price	✓
VAT rate	
Total	✓

Feedback: The total does not cast correctly.

146 NORMAN PRICE & CO

(a)

Daybook	✓
Sales daybook	
Purchases daybook	✓
Cashbook	
Purchase returns daybook	
Sales returns daybook	
Discounts allowed daybook	

(b)

Date 20XX	Supplier	Invoice number	Net £	VAT £	Total £
8 Mar	Norris Ltd	3897	1,010.00	202.00	1,212.00
10 Mar	Sam Jones	0187	878.40	175.68	1,054.08
11 Mar	James & Sarah Ltd	402929	463.80	92.76	556.56
11 Mar	Trevor Dylis Ltd	73910	1,329.10	265.82	1,594.92
14 Mar	Henry's Office Supplies	7208	584.00	116.80	700.80
		Totals	4,265.30	853.06	5,118.36

(c)

Discrepancy	✓
Prompt payment discount value	
VAT	✓
Invoice number	✓
Total	

Feedback: The VAT should be £2.70 calculated as £135 × 2% or £13.50 × 20%

147 FREDDIE LTD

Purchases daybook

Date 20XX	Details	Invoice number	Total £	VAT £	Net £	Product 14211 £	Product 14212 £
31 July	Box Ltd	2177	960	160	800	800	
31 July	Shrew Ltd	2175	14,400	2,400	12,000	12,000	
31 July	Novot & Co	2176	4,800	800	4,000		4,000
	Totals		20,160	3,360	16,800	12,800	4,000

148 ALPHA LTD

(a)

Purchase return £900

(b)

Invoice 486

(c)

£8,580.00

149 MAXIMUS LTD

(a)

<table>
<tr><td colspan="3" align="center">Alpha Ltd

121 Baker St

Newcastle, NE1 7DJ

REMITTANCE ADVICE</td></tr>
<tr><td colspan="2">To: Maximus Ltd 20XX</td><td>Date: 31 Aug</td></tr>
<tr><td colspan="3">Please find attached our cheque in payment of the following amounts.</td></tr>
<tr><td align="center">Invoice number</td><td align="center">Credit note number</td><td align="center">Amount
£</td></tr>
<tr><td align="center">864</td><td></td><td align="center">6,386</td></tr>
<tr><td></td><td align="center">252</td><td align="center">964</td></tr>
<tr><td></td><td align="center">258</td><td align="center">1,218</td></tr>
<tr><td></td><td></td><td></td></tr>
<tr><td></td><td></td><td></td></tr>
<tr><td></td><td align="right">Total amount paid</td><td align="center">4,204</td></tr>
</table>

(b)   A remittance note is for our records only   F

A remittance note is sent to a supplier to advise them of the amount being paid   T

150 HOLLY LTD

(a)

| Purchase return 286 |

(b)

| £928.80 |

(c)

| £172.00 |

(d)

| £1,032.00 |

151 EP MANUFACTURERS

(a)

| Cheque for £1,200 |

(b)

| Invoice 488 |

(c)

| £4,850.00 |

152 STANNY LTD

(a)

Ringo Rings

37 Parker Lane

Stoke SK1 0KE

REMITTANCE ADVICE

To: Stanny Ltd   **Date:** 31 Mar 20XX

Please find attached our cheque in payment of the following amounts.

Invoice number	Credit note number	Amount £
694		2,300
658		3,640
	198	650
	154	1,250
	Total amount paid	**4,040**

(b)   A remittance note is for our and the suppliers records   T

A remittance note is sent by a supplier confirming amounts received from them   F

153 TOYWORLD

(a)

Cheque for £500

Picklist: Invoice 207, Invoice 310, Invoice 504, Invoice 505, Cheque for £3,400, Cheque for £500

(b)

Invoice 505

Picklist: Invoice 207, Invoice 310, Invoice 504, Invoice 505, Cheque for £3,400, Cheque for £500

(c)

£4,000

154 HENRY HOUSE

(a)

<table>
<tr><td colspan="3" align="center">**Henry House**
22 Nursery Road
Keighley, BD22 7BD

REMITTANCE ADVICE</td></tr>
<tr><td colspan="3">**To:** Abbies Party</td></tr>
<tr><td colspan="3">**Date:** 31 August 20XX</td></tr>
<tr><td colspan="3">Please find attached our cheque in payment of the following amounts.</td></tr>
<tr><td align="center">**Invoice number**</td><td align="center">**Credit note number**</td><td align="center">**Amount**
£</td></tr>
<tr><td align="center">242</td><td></td><td align="center">220</td></tr>
<tr><td></td><td align="center">27</td><td align="center">82</td></tr>
<tr><td></td><td></td><td></td></tr>
<tr><td></td><td></td><td></td></tr>
<tr><td></td><td align="center">**Total amount paid**</td><td align="center">138</td></tr>
</table>

(b)

D The remittance advice note will be sent to the supplier to advise them of the amount being paid

155 GREY GARAGES

Remittance advice			
To: Mulberry Motors			
From: Grey Garages			
Payment method: BACS		**Date of payment:** 25 July	

Items outstanding			Tick if included in payment
Date 20XX	**Details**	**Amount £**	
23-Jun	Invoice 213	740	✓
06-Jul	Credit note 14	120	✓
13-Jul	Invoice 216	620	✓
19-Jul	Invoice 257	870	
Total amount paid			£1,240

156 ERRICO

Supplier	£	Date by which the payment should be received by the supplier
Giacomo	67.51	11 June 20XX
Gaetani	39.33	9 June 20XX

157 LEWIN & CO

(a)

Supplier	£	Date by which the payment should be received by the supplier
Bridge Brothers	110.25	23rd October
Mitchells	128.79	24th October

(b)

Xcess Stock Unit 7 Windy Industrial Estate Irvine, KA6 8HU To: Lewin & Co Date: 31 Dec 20XX			Not to be paid
Date 20XX	Details	Transaction amount £	
12 Dec	Invoice 1001	1,700	
13 Dec	Invoice 1003	1,500	✓
21 Dec	Invoice 1004	2,350	
21 Dec	Credit note 101	940	
22 Dec	Invoice 1005	450	✓
27 Dec	Invoice 1010	470	
28 Dec	Credit note 102	50	✓

(c)

£3,580

(d)

£1,516

158 ASHBOURNE LTD

(a)

Supplier name	Invoice amount £	Invoice date 20XX	Amount to be paid £	Date by which supplier should receive payment
Kennack & Co	756.90	9 Jan	756.90	8 February
Butterworth & Sons	1,317.83	11 Jan	1,317.83	10 February
Jermyn Ltd	847.60	10 Jan	805.22	17 January

Feedback: Only Jermyn Ltd should be paid early as the others do not offer discounts of 5% or more. The payment will be £847.60 × 95% = £805.22

(b)

Transactions	✓
Opening balance	✓
Invoice 287	✓
Invoice 294	
Invoice 304	✓
Invoice 307	
Invoice 307	
Credit note 045	
Invoice 342	

Feedback: The payment of £5,296 = £639 + £1,204 + £3,453.

(c)

Type of error	✓
Underpayment	
Overpayment	
Missing transactions	
Duplicate transaction	✓
Timing difference	

Feedback: Invoice 307 is recorded twice.

159 FARFIELD LTD

(a)

Supplier name	Invoice amount £	Invoice date 20XX	Amount to be paid £	Date by which supplier should receive payment
Archer Joinery	1,340.00	25 Aug	1,340.00	30 September
Sankey Electrical	4,372.80	26 Aug	4,263.48	9 September
Pannal Construction	3,720.00	26 Aug	3,608.40	5 September

(b)

Transactions	✓
Opening balance	✓
Invoice 308	
Invoice 314	✓
Credit note 048	✓
Invoice 326	
Invoice 338	
Invoice 343	

Feedback: the cheque for £1,605 = £1,160 + £1,342 − £897

(c)

Type of error	✓
Underpayment	
Timing difference	✓
Overpayment	
Missing transactions	
Duplicate transaction	

Feedback: The difference of £896 relates to CHQ 0786 which was presumably sent by Farfield Ltd before the month end but received by Kelham builders on 2 October.

Section 6

ANSWERS TO PRACTICE QUESTIONS

POBC L01 USE CONTROL ACCOUNTS

160 MONSTER MUNCHIES

(a)

Details	Amount £	Debit ✓	Credit ✓
Balance of receivables at 1 June	48,000	✓	
Goods sold on credit	12,415	✓	
Receipts from credit customers	22,513		✓
Discount allowed	465		✓
Sales returns from credit customers	320		✓

(b)

Dr £37,117	✓

(c)

	£
Receivables ledger control account balance as at 30 June	37,117
Total of subsidiary (receivables) ledger accounts as at 30 June	36,797
Difference	320

(d)

Sales returns may have been omitted from the subsidiary ledger.	
Discounts allowed may have been omitted from the subsidiary ledger.	
Sales returns may have been entered in the subsidiary ledger twice.	✓
Discounts allowed may have been entered in the subsidiary ledger twice.	✓

(e)

Reconciliation of the receivables ledger control account assures managers that the amount showing as owed to suppliers is correct.	
Reconciliation of the receivables ledger control account assures managers that the amount showing as outstanding from customers is correct.	✓
Reconciliation of the receivables ledger control account will show if a purchase invoice has been omitted from the payables ledger.	
Reconciliation of the receivables ledger control account will show if a purchase invoice has been omitted from the receivables ledger.	

161 JACK'S BOX

(a)

Details	Amount £	Debit ✓	Credit ✓
Balance of receivables at 1 April	60,589	✓	
Goods sold on credit	26,869	✓	
Payments received from credit customers	29,411		✓
Discount allowed	598		✓
Goods returned from credit customers	1,223		✓

(b)

Dr £55,030	
Cr £55,030	
Dr £56,226	✓
Cr £56,226	
Dr £52,584	
Cr £52,584	

(c)

	£
Receivables Ledger control account balances as at 30 April	56,226
Total of subsidiary (receivables) ledger accounts as at 30 April	55,003
Difference	1,223

(d) ✓

Sales returns may have been omitted from the subsidiary ledger.	
Discounts allowed may have been omitted from the subsidiary ledger.	
Sales returns have been entered into the subsidiary ledger twice.	✓
Discounts allowed have been entered into receivables ledger control account twice	

(e) ✓

Reconciliation of the receivables ledger control account will show if a purchase invoice has been omitted from the payables ledger.	
Reconciliation of the receivables ledger control account will show if a sales invoice has been omitted from the payables ledger.	
Reconciliation of the receivables ledger control account assures managers that the amount showing due to suppliers is correct.	
Reconciliation of the receivables ledger control account assures managers that the amount showing due from customers is correct.	✓

162 CILLA'S SINKS

(a)

Details	Amount £	Debit ✓	Credit ✓
Balance of payables at 1 June	52,150		✓
Goods bought on credit	19,215		✓
Payments made to credit suppliers	19,073	✓	
Discount received	284	✓	
Goods returned to credit suppliers	1,023	✓	

(b)

Cr £50,985	✓

(c)

	£
Payables ledger control account balance as at 30 June	50,985
Total of subsidiary (payable) ledger accounts as at 30 June	52,008
Difference	1,023

(d)

Goods returned may have been omitted from the subsidiary ledger.	✓
Discounts received may have been omitted from the subsidiary ledger.	
Goods returned may have been entered in the subsidiary ledger twice.	
Discounts received may have been entered into the subsidiary ledger twice.	

(e)

Reconciliation of the PLCA will help to identify any supplier invoices that have been omitted in error.	✓
Reconciliation of the payables ledger control account will show if a sales invoice has been omitted from the payables ledger.	
Reconciliation of the payables ledger control account will show if a sales invoice has been omitted from the receivables ledger.	
Reconciliation of the payables ledger control account will help to identify any discounts allowed that have been omitted in error.	

163 VIK'S TRICKS

(a)

Details	Amount £	Debit ✓	Credit ✓
Balance of receivables at 1 June	58,120	✓	
Goods sold on credit	20,013	✓	
Receipts from credit customers	22,327		✓
Discount allowed	501		✓
Sales returns from credit customers	970		✓

(b)

Dr £54,335	✓

(c)

	£
Receivables ledger control account balance as at 30 June	54,335
Total of subsidiary (receivables) ledger accounts as at 30 June	55,305
Difference	970

(d)

Discounts allowed may have been entered in the subsidiary ledger twice.	
Discounts allowed may have been omitted from the subsidiary ledger.	✓
Sales returns may have been entered in the subsidiary ledger twice.	
Sales returns may have been omitted from the subsidiary ledger.	✓

(e)

Reconciliation of the receivables ledger control account will help to identify any customer invoices that have been omitted in error.	✓
Reconciliation of the receivables ledger control account will show if a purchase invoice has been omitted from the receivables ledger.	
Reconciliation of the receivables ledger control account will show if a purchase invoice has been omitted from the payables ledger.	
Reconciliation of the receivables ledger control account will help to identify any discounts received that have been omitted in error.	

164 ZHANG

(a)

RLCA

Details	Amount £	Details	Amount £
Balance b/d	65,830	SBD overcast	1,200
		Discount given	210
		Balance c/d	64,420
	65,830		**65,830**
Balance b/d	64,420		

List of balances:

	£
Total:	65,090
Contra missing	(800)
Credit note posted twice	130
Revised total:	64,420

(b) **Show whether the following statements are true or false:**

	True ✓	False ✓
An aged trade receivables analysis is used when chasing customers for outstanding payments.	✓	
An aged trade receivables analysis is sent to credit customers when payments are being requested.		✓

165 HANDYSIDE

(a)

PLCA

Details	Amount £	Details	Amount £
Returns	120	Balance b/d	25,360
		Missing invoice	720
Balance c/d	25,960		
	26,080		**26,080**
		Balance b/d	25,960

List of balances:

	£
Total	26,000
Net amount entered	400
Returns	(350)
Transposition error	(90)
Revised total	25,960

(b) **Show whether the following statements are true or false:**

	True ✓	False ✓
The payables ledger control account enables a business to see how much is owed to individual suppliers		✓
The payables ledger control account total should reconcile to the total of the list of supplier balances in the payables ledger	✓	

166 RING TELEPHONE

(a)

VAT control

Details	Amount £	Details	Amount £
Sales returns	360	Sales	30,600
Purchases	16,200	Cash sales	48
		Purchases returns	1,160
Balance c/d	15,248		
	31,808		**31,808**
		Balance b/d	15,248

(b)   No – it is £15,248 owed **to** HMRC

(c)

	£	Debit	Credit
Balance brought down	38,900	✓	

Workings:

VAT control

Details	Amount £	Details	Amount £
Debit balances	93,800	Credit balances	54,400
Purchase of equipment	400	Cash sales	900
		Balance c/d	38,900
	94,200		**94,200**
Balance b/d	38,900		

167 JO'S JOINERS

(a)

VAT Control

Details	Amount £	Details	Amount £
Purchases	21,000	Sales	31,200
Sales returns	720	Cash sales	120
		Purchases returns	1,088
Balance c/d	10,688		
	32,408		**32,408**
		Balance b/d	10,688

(b)   Yes

168 PHILIP'S CABINS

(a)

VAT control

Details	Amount £	Details	Amount £
Sales returns	600	Sales	35,960
Purchases	20,040	Cash sales	112
		Purchases returns	1,144
Balance c/d	16,576		
	37,216		**37,216**
		Balance b/d	16,576

(b) No – the amount owed to HMRC is £16,576.

169 DISLEY

(a)

	£	Debit	Credit
VAT total in the sales day book	65,420		65,420
VAT total in the purchases day book	21,340	21,340	
VAT total in the sales returns day book	480	480	
VAT balance brought forward, owed to HMRC	24,910		24,910
VAT on irrecoverable debts	830	830	
VAT on petty cash expenses paid	210	210	

(b) No – the amount owed to HMRC is £67,470.

(c)

	£	Debit	Credit
Balance brought down	19,730		✓

Workings:

VAT control

Details	Amount £	Details	Amount £
Debit balances	42,300	Credit balances	61,250
Irrecoverable debt	200	Discounts received	980
Balance c/d	19,730		
	62,230		**62,230**
		Balance b/d	19,730

170 KERR

(a) **Show whether each item is a debit or credit balance by copying the amount into the correct column**

	£	Debit	Credit
VAT total in the purchase returns day book	1,320		1,320
VAT total in discounts received day book	400		400
VAT on cash purchases	2,670	2,670	
VAT on the sale of equipment	970		970
VAT total in discounts allowed day book	500	500	
VAT refund received from HMRC	2,580		2,580
VAT on cash sales	5,880		5,880
VAT balance brought forward, due from HMRC	2,580	2,580	

(b) Yes – the amount owed is correct

171 NEILSON

(a)

	£	Debit	Credit
VAT total in the sales day book	54,670		54,670
VAT total in the purchases day book	26,340	26,340	
VAT total in the sales returns day book	1,240	1,240	
VAT total in the purchases returns day book	760		760
VAT on sale of equipment	3,210		3,210
VAT on petty cash expenses paid	500	500	
VAT balance brought forward, owed to HMRC	42,180		42,180
VAT on irrecoverable debts	430	430	
VAT paid to HMRC during the period	32,150	32,150	
VAT on cash sales	6,540		6,540
VAT on cash purchases	7,520	7,520	
VAT total in discounts allowed day book	1,130	1,130	
VAT total in discounts received day book	980		980

(b) Yes – the amount owed is correct

POBC LO2 RECONCILE A BANK STATEMENT WITH THE CASH BOOK

172 BLOSSOM BLOOMS

(a)

Checks to be made	Cheque	Telephone credit card payment ✓
Check expiry date	✓	
Check issue number	✓	✓
Check not post dated		✓
Check security number	✓	
Check words and figures match		✓
Check card has not been tampered with	✓	✓

(b) When Blossom Blooms makes payments to suppliers by debit card, the amount paid affects the bank current account

True

When Blossom Blooms makes payments to suppliers by credit card, the amount paid affects the bank current account

False

173 PETE'S PARROTS

(a)

Checks to be made	Cheque ✓	Telephone credit card payment ✓
Check expiry date		✓
Check issue number		
Check not posted dated	✓	
Check security number		✓
Check words and figures match	✓	
Check card has not been tampered with		

(b) When Pete's Parrots makes payments to suppliers by credit card, the amount does not leave the bank current account immediately

True

When Pete's Parrots makes payments to suppliers by debit card, the amount paid affects the bank current account

True

174   BANK EFFECTS 1

Which TWO balances will NOT reduce funds in the bank balance of the payer at the date of payment?

Standing order	
Cheque payment	✓
CHAPS payment	
Credit card payment	✓

175   BANK EFFECTS 2

Which THREE balances WILL reduce funds in the bank balance of the payer at the date of payment?

Direct debit	✓
Building society cheque payment	
Debit card payment	✓
BACS payment	✓

176   METHODS OF PAYMENT 1

Match the payment need with the most likely method of payment to be used.

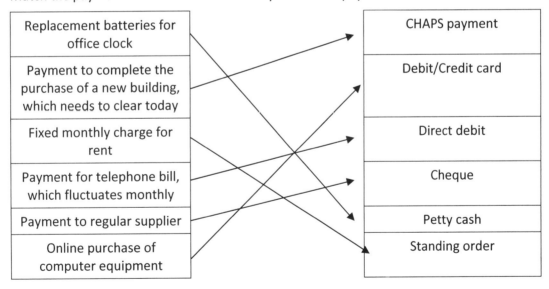

Replacement batteries for office clock	CHAPS payment
Payment to complete the purchase of a new building, which needs to clear today	Debit/Credit card
Fixed monthly charge for rent	Direct debit
Payment for telephone bill, which fluctuates monthly	Cheque
Payment to regular supplier	Petty cash
Online purchase of computer equipment	Standing order

177 METHODS OF PAYMENT 2

Match the payment with the description below

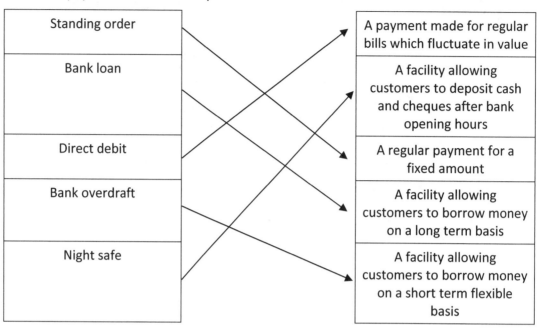

178 RIVERS LTD

(a) – (c)

Date 20XX	Details	Bank £	Date 20XX	Cheque number	Details	Bank £
01 June	Balance b/d	3,115	01 June	111013	Indigo Beds	650
17 June	Bracken Ltd	300	01 June	111014	DirectFit	1,420
21 June	Airfleet Interiors	560	01 June	111015	Langdon	60
22 June	Harris Homes	333	01 June	111016	QPF Ltd	615
12 June	Ayreshire Build	970	02 June	111017	OMD Ltd	815
23 June	Bank interest	15	02 June	111018	Hamden Ltd	450
			13 June	111019	Freeman & Cope	522
			13 June		Collins	175
			20 June		Rent	500
			23 June		Bank charges	20
			23 June		Balance c/d	66
		5,293				5,293
24 June	Balance b/d	66				

179   LUXURY BATHROOMS

(a) – (c)

Date	Details	Bank	Date	Cheque	Details	Bank
01 April	Balance b/d	17,845	01 April	120045	R Sterling Ltd	8,850
19 April	Olsen & Lane	2,150	01 April	120046	Bert Cooper	2,250
22 April	Frith Ltd	685	01 April	120047	Hetko & Sons	64
22 April	Hodgetts & Co	282	02 April	120048	Barrett Ltd	3,256
04 April	Ricketts & Co	465	02 April	120049	K Plomer	542
			08 April	120050	I&E Brown	655
			08 April	120051	T Roberts	1,698
			14 April		AMB Ltd	2,265
			14 April		D Draper	2,950
			22 April		Bank charges	63
			23 April		Overdraft fee	25
24 April	Balance c/d	1,191				
		22,618				22,618
			25 April		Balance b/d	1,191

180   WHOLESALE FLOORING

(a) – (c)

Date 20XX	Details	Bank £	Date 20XX	Cheque number	Details	Bank £
			01 June		Balance b/d	5,125
16 June	Beeston's	550	01 June	104373	Good Iron	890
19 June	Airfleet Exteriors	3,025	01 June	104374	Ashworth and Co	1,725
22 June	Jones's	2,775	01 June	104375	Ironfit	210
12 June	Aintree and Co	1,250	05 June	104376	OSS Ltd	1,275
			07 June	104377	Perfect Tools	725
			08 June	104378	Campden Ltd	784
			14 June	104379	Thornley and Thwaite	675
			14 June	104380	Castle and Cove	178
			20 June		MD County Council	400
			23 June		Bank charges	160
23 June	Balance c/d	4,637	23 June		Overdraft fee	90
		12,237				12,237
			24 June		Balance b/d	4,637

181 24 HOUR TAXIS

(a) – (c)

Date 20XX	Details	Bank £	Date 20XX	Cheque number	Details	Bank £
01 June	Balance b/d	6,025	01 June	102597	Best Ideas	910
18 June	Earnshaw's	1,000	02 June	102598	Bentley and Burn	2,010
19 June	Mainstreet Ltd	1,206	02 June	102599	Bits and Bats	315
21 June	Housley Inc	1,725	03 June	102600	LPF Ltd	1,725
12 June	Barron Homes	1,475	07 June	102601	Essentials	686
			08 June	102602	Hopburn Ltd	675
			15 June	102603	Thistle Tools	410
			15 June	102604	C Campbell Ltd	275
			20 June		AB Insurance	1,250
			23 June		Bank charges	50
			23 June		Overdraft fee	25
			23 June		Balance c/d	3,100
		11,431				11,431
24 June	Balance b/d	3,100				

182 WOOD

(a) – (c)

Date 20XX	Details	Bank £	Date 20XX	Cheque number	Details	Bank £
01 June	Balance b/d	17,640				
03 June	Bradley	1,320	04 June	110341	Carr	1,540
03 June	Cash sales	9,420	04 June	110342	Ramsden	980
03 June	Thanoj	2,450	04 June	110343	Coulson	750
21 June	Cash sales	7,430	04 June	110344	Brodie	570
21 June	Devitt	1,990	04 June	110345	Jones	550
17 June	Interest earned	80	04 June	110346	Gritton	740
			20 June		Bore	250
			12 June		Southwell	820
			20 June		Direct Debit Blundell	400
			23 June		Balance c/d	33,730
		40,330				40,330
24 June	Balance b/d	33,730				

183   PEARSON

(a) – (c)

Date 20XX	Details	Bank £	Date 20XX	Cheque number	Details	Bank £
01 June	Balance b/d	550	07 June	110123	Connell	430
09 June	Cash sales	840	07 June	110124	Renner	720
14 June	Cash sales	1,540	07 June	110125	Bond	750
22 June	Cunnington	1,730	07 June	110126	Hatton	75
02 June	Interest received	5	07 June	110127	Bull	270
			07 June	110128	Black	135
			07 June	110129	Southall	740
			02 June		McMenemy	1,200
			20 June		Findus	300
			23 June		Bank charges	25
			23 June		Balance c/d	20
		4,665				4,665
24 June	Balance b/d	20				

184   MCKEOWN

(a) – (c)

Date 20XX	Details	Bank £	Date 20XX	Cheque number	Details	Bank £
01 June	Balance b/d	7,180	07 June	110157	Williams	430
12 June	Sherwood	640	07 June	110158	Forecast	520
14 June	Cash sales	1,200	07 June	110159	Beasant	1,240
22 June	Tweedy	860	07 June	110160	Davison	1,420
23 June	Butterwood	440	07 June	110161	Mildenhall	750
01 June	Interest received	85	23 June		Wilmott	300
20 June	Coyne	1,630				
23 June	Interest received	35				
			23 June		Balance c/d	7,410
		12,070				12,070
24 June	Balance b/d	7,410				

185 RIVERS BANK RECONCILIATION

Balance per bank statement	£510
Add:	
Name: Airfleet Interiors	£560
Name: Harris Homes	£333
Total to add	£893
Less:	
Name: OMD Ltd	£815
Name: Freeman & Cope	£522
Total to subtract	£1,337
Balance as per cash book	£66

186 LUXURY BATHROOMS BANK RECONCILIATION

Balance per bank statement	£82
Add:	
Name: Frith Ltd	£685
Name: Hodgetts & Co	£282
Total to add	£967
Less:	
Name: K Plomer	£542
Name: T Roberts	£1,698
Total to subtract	£2,240
Balance as per cash book	(£1,191)

187 WHOLESALE FLOORING BANK RECONCILIATION

Balance per bank statement	(£9,584)
Add:	
Name: Airfleet Exteriors	£3,025
Name: Jones's	£2,775
Total to add	£5,800
Less:	
Name: Thornley & Thwaite	£675
Name: Castle & Cove	£178
Total to subtract	£853
Balance as per cash book	(£4,637)

188   24 HOUR TAXIS BANK RECONCILIATION

Balance per bank statement	£854
Add:	
Name: Mainstreet Ltd	£1,206
Name: Housley Inc	£1,725
Total to add	£2,931
Less:	
Name: Thistle Tools	£410
Name: C Campbell Ltd	£275
Total to subtract	£685
Balance as per cash book	£3,100

189   WOOD BANK RECONCILIATION

(a)

Balance per bank statement	£25,840
Add:	
Name: Cash sales	£7,430
Name: Devitt	£1,990
Total to add	£9,420
Less:	
Name: Ramsden	£980
Name: Jones	£550
Total to subtract	£1,530
Balance as per cash book	£33,730

(b)

Balance carried down	Bank column totals
£	£
33,730	40,330

Working:

Cash book

Date 20XX	Details	Bank £	Date 20XX	Cheque number	Details	Bank £
01 June	Balance b/d	17,640				
03 June	Bradley	1,320	04 June	110341	Carr	1,540
03 June	Cash sales	9,420	04 June	110342	Ramsden	980
03 June	Thanoj	2,450	04 June	110343	Coulson	750
21 June	Cash sales	7,430	04 June	110344	Brodie	570
21 June	Devitt	1,990	04 June	110345	Jones	550
17 June	Interest earned	80	04 June	110346	Gritton	740
			20 June		Bore	250
			12 June		Southwell	820
			20 June		Direct Debit Blundell	400
			23 June		Balance c/d	33,730
		40,330				40,330
24 June	Balance b/d	33,730				

190 PEARSON BANK RECONCILIATION

(a)

Balance per bank statement	(£105)
Add:	
Name: Cunnington	£1,730
Total to add	**£1,730**
Less:	
Name: Renner	£720
Name: Bond	£750
Name: Black	£135
Total to subtract	**£1,605**
Balance as per cash book	**£20**

(b) Show which security procedure listed below Pearson should use to ensure the security of receipts from customers.

	✓
Cash received from customers should be kept in a locked safe until banked	✓
Cash should be banked on a monthly basis	
Cheques received too late to bank should be posted through the bank's letter box	

191 MCKEOWN BANK RECONCILIATION

(a)

Balance per bank statement	£8,770
Add:	
Name: Tweedy	£860
Name: Butterwood	£440
Total to add	**£1,300**
Less:	
Name: Beasant	£1,240
Name: Davison	£1,420
Total to subtract	**£2,660**
Balance as per cash book	**£7,410**

(b)

Balance carried down £	Bank column totals £
7,410	12,070

Workings:

Cash book

Date 20XX	Details	Bank £	Date 20XX	Cheque number	Details	Bank £
01 June	Balance b/d	7,180	07 June	110157	Williams	430
12 June	Sherwood	640	07 June	110158	Forecast	520
14 June	Cash sales	1,200	07 June	110159	Beasant	1,240
22 June	Tweedy	860	07 June	110160	Davison	1,420
23 June	Butterwood	440	07 June	110161	Mildenhall	750
01 June	Interest received	85	23 June		Wilmott	300
20 June	Coyne	1,630				
23 June	Interest received	35				
			23 June		Balance c/d	7,410
		12,070				12,070
24 June	Balance b/d	7,410				

POBC L03 USE THE JOURNAL

192 INTREPID INTERIORS

(a)

Account name	Amount £	Debit ✓	Credit ✓
Cash at bank	7,250	✓	
Bank Loan	5,000		✓
Capital	10,625		✓
Motor vehicles	4,750	✓	
Insurances	575	✓	
Stationery	300	✓	
Sundry expenses	225	✓	
Motor expenses	135	✓	
Advertising	990	✓	
Rent and rates	1,400	✓	

(b)

Recording of a contra

193 BEDROOM BITS

(a)

Account name	Amount £	Debit ✓	Credit ✓
Cash	325	✓	
Cash at bank	9,625	✓	
Capital	22,008		✓
Fixtures and fittings	4,250	✓	
Insurance	1,050	✓	
Loan from bank	15,000		✓
Miscellaneous expenses	413	✓	
Motor vehicle	19,745	✓	
Office expenses	350	✓	
Rent and rates	1,250	✓	

(b)

Irrecoverable debt written off

194 GARDEN GATES

Account name	Amount £	Debit ✓	Credit ✓
Cash	450	✓	
Cash at bank	11,125	✓	
Capital	28,941		✓
Plant and machinery	5,050	✓	
Insurance	990	✓	
Loan from bank	12,500		✓
General office expenses	378	✓	
Motor vehicle	20,755	✓	

195 IVANO

(a)

	Amount £
Net pay (2,400 – 480 – 245 – 80)	1,595

Note: The net pay is the gross pay less all the EMPLOYEE'S deductions. Employer's NIC is not part of this calculation.

(b)

	Amount £
Wages and salaries (Employer's expense) (2,400 Gross pay + 255 Employer's NIC)	2,655

(c)

	Amount £
Liabilities (HMRC and Pension) HMRC = 480 + 245 + 255 = 980 Pension = 80	1,060

196 ANNA

(a)

	Amount £
Net pay (1,400 − 280 − 125 − 60)	935

Note: The net pay is the gross pay less all the EMPLOYEE'S deductions. Employer's NIC is not part of this calculation.

(b)

	Amount £
Wages and salaries (Employer's expense) (1,400 Gross pay + 135 Employer's NIC + 70 Employer pension contributions)	1,605

(c)

	Amount £
Liabilities (HMRC and pension) HMRC = 280 + 125 + 135 = 540 Pension = 130	670

197 GROSS PAY 1

Item	Added to gross pay ✓	Not added to gross pay ✓
Trade Union subscription		✓
Employer's NIC	✓	
Employee's Pension		✓
Employer's Pension	✓	
Employee's NIC		✓

The wages expense comprises the employee's gross pay plus any contributions made by the employer, in this case pension and NIC. Trade Union subscription would be deducted from the employee's gross pay and paid to the Trade Union.

198 GROSS PAY 2

Item	Deducted from gross pay ✓	Not deducted from gross pay ✓
Employer's NIC		✓
Commission		✓
Employee's NIC	✓	
Employee pension contribution	✓	
PAYE	✓	

Gross pay is the amount the employee has earned from working for the company and therefore includes commission. Employer's NIC is added to gross pay in order to calculate the total wages expense for the company.

199 A POCKET FULL OF POSES

(i)

Account name	Amount £	Debit ✓	Credit ✓
Wages expense	17,755	✓	
Wages control	17,755		✓

(ii)

Account name	Amount £	Debit ✓	Credit ✓
Wages control	7,500	✓	
HMRC	7,500		✓

(iii)

Account name	Amount £	Debit ✓	Credit ✓
Wages control	8,405	✓	
Bank	8,405		✓

(iv)

Account name	Amount £	Debit ✓	Credit ✓
Wages control	1,850	✓	
Pension	1,850		✓

Proof (not required to answer the question correctly):

Wages control

HM Revenue and Customs	7,500	Wages expense	17,755
Bank	8,405		
Pension	1,850		
	_____		_____
	17,755		17,755
	_____		_____

200 RHYME TIME

(i)

Account name	Amount £	Debit ✓	Credit ✓
Wages expense	11,915	✓	
Wages control	11,915		✓

(ii)

Account name	Amount £	Debit ✓	Credit ✓
Wages control	5,026	✓	
HMRC	5,026		✓

(iii)

Account name	Amount £	Debit ✓	Credit ✓
Wages control	5,739	✓	
Bank	5,739		✓

(iv)

Account name	Amount £	Debit ✓	Credit ✓
Wages control	1,150	✓	
Pension	1,150		✓

Proof (not required to answer the question correctly):

Wages control

HMRC	5,026	Wages expense	11,915
Bank	5,739		
Pension	1,150		
	_____		_____
	11,915		11,915
	_____		_____

201 DOWN & OUT

(i)

Account name	Amount £	Debit ✓	Credit ✓
Wages expense	9,567	✓	
Wages control	9,567		✓

(ii)

Account name	Amount £	Debit ✓	Credit ✓
Wages control	3,673	✓	
HMRC	3,673		✓

(iii)

Account name	Amount £	Debit ✓	Credit ✓
Wages control	5,469	✓	
Bank	5,469		✓

(iv)

Account name	Amount £	Debit ✓	Credit ✓
Wages control	425	✓	
Trade union	425		✓

Proof (not required to answer the question correctly):

Wages control

HMRC	3,673	Wages expense	9,567
Bank	5,469		
Trade union	425		
	─────		─────
	9,567		9,567
	─────		─────

202 DEV

(i)

Account name	Amount £	Debit ✓	Credit ✓
Wages expense	13,963	✓	
Wages control	13,963		✓

(ii)

Account name	Amount £	Debit ✓	Credit ✓
Wages control	6,251	✓	
HMRC	6,251		✓

(iii)

Account name	Amount £	Debit ✓	Credit ✓
Wages control	7,212	✓	
Bank	7,212		✓

(iv)

Account name	Amount £	Debit ✓	Credit ✓
Wages control	500	✓	
Trade union	500		✓

Proof (not required to answer the question correctly):

Wages control

HMRC	6,251	Wages expense	13,963
Bank	7,212		
Trade Union	500		
	———		———
	13,963		13,963
	———		———

203 BEDROOM BITS

Account name	Amount £	Debit ✓	Credit ✓
Irrecoverable debts	2,000	✓	
VAT	400	✓	
Receivables ledger control	2,400		✓

204 GARDEN GATES

Account name	Amount £	Debit ✓	Credit ✓
Irrecoverable debts	2,600	✓	
VAT	520	✓	
Receivables ledger control	3,120		✓

205 CHESTNUT

RLCA

Details	Amount £	Details	Amount £
Balance b/d	46,000	Contra	4,000
		Balance c/d	42,000
	46,000		**46,000**
Balance b/d	42,000		

PLCA

Details	Amount £	Details	Amount £
Contra	4,000	Balance b/d	31,000
Balance c/d	27,000		
	31,000		**31,000**
		Balance b/d	27,000

206 ALLEN

RLCA

Details	Amount £	Details	Amount £
Balance b/d	56,000	Contra	11,000
		Balance c/d	45,000
	56,000		**56,000**
Balance b/d	45,000		

PLCA

Details	Amount £	Details	Amount £
Contra	11,000	Balance b/d	49,000
Balance c/d	38,000		
	49,000		**49,000**
		Balance b/d	38,000

207 BEANZ

Account name	Amount £	Debit ✓	Credit ✓
Irrecoverable debts	4,350	✓	
VAT	870	✓	
Receivables ledger control	5,220		✓

208 ERROR TYPES 1

Error in the general ledger	Error disclosed by the trial balance	Error NOT disclosed by the trial balance
Incorrectly calculating the balance on the Motor Vehicles account.	✓	
Recording a receipt for commission received in the bank interest received account.		✓
Recording a bank receipt for bank interest received on the debit side of both the bank account and the bank interest received account.	✓	
Recording supplier invoices on the debit side of the payables ledger control account and the credit side of the purchases account.		✓
Recording a payment by cheque to a payable in the payables ledger control account only.	✓	
Recording a bank payment of £124 for insurance as £142 in the insurance account and £124 in the bank account.	✓	

209 ERROR TYPES 2

Error in the general ledger	Would cause imbalance	Would NOT cause imbalance
Recording a bank receipt for rent received on the credit side of both the bank account and rent received account.	✓	
Recording a payment for new machinery in the equipment hire account.		✓
Recording a purchase return on the credit side of the payables ledger control account and the debit side of the purchase returns account.		✓
Incorrectly calculating the balance on the bank interest received account.	✓	
Recording a payment by cheque to a payable in the bank account only.	✓	
Recording a bank payment of £120 for stationery as £210 in both accounts.		✓

210 ERROR TYPES 3

Error in the general ledger	Type of error
Recording a bank receipt for rent received on the credit side of both the bank account and rent received account.	Two entries on one side
Recording a payment for new machinery in the equipment hire account.	Error of principle
Recording a purchase return on the credit side of the payables ledger control account and the debit side of the purchase returns account.	Reversal of entries

211 ERROR TYPES 4

Error in the general ledger	Type of error
Recording a payment by cheque to a payable in the bank account only.	Single entry
Recording a bank payment of £100 for stationery as £210 in both accounts.	Error of original entry
Recording a receipt for commission received in the bank interest received account.	Error of commission

212 ERROR TYPES 5

Error in the general ledger	Type of error
A credit sale made at the month end was not recorded.	Error of omission
Recording a bank payment of £120 for stationery as £210 in the stationery account and correctly in the bank account.	Transposition error
Recording a receipt for commission received in the PLCA.	Error of principle

213 ERROR TYPES 6

Error in the general ledger	Would cause imbalance ✓
Forgetting to post a journal to record a contra.	
Posting the VAT on a sale transaction as a debit rather than a credit.	✓
Recording a cash purchase in purchases and VAT only.	✓
Recording the electricity expense as a debit to wages expenses, with the corresponding entry correctly credited to cash.	

214 PRINCIPLES

(a)

Recording a bank payment for rent on the debit side of the office equipment account.	✓

(b)

Recording rent received as a debit in the rent account.	✓

215 EXTRACTION

(a)

Totalling the sales day book correctly but entering into the RLCA as a credit balance.	✓

(b)

Posting a £200 invoice for electricity as £210 in both the electricity and bank account.	✓

216 BANK ERROR

(i)

Account name	Amount £	Debit ✓	Credit ✓
Repairs	750	✓	
Bank	750		✓

(ii)

Account name	Amount £	Debit ✓	Credit ✓
Repairs	750	✓	
Bank	750		✓

217 RENT ERROR

(i)

Account name	Amount £	Debit ✓	Credit ✓
Bank	500	✓	
Rent received	500		✓

(ii)

Account name	Amount £	Debit ✓	Credit ✓
Bank	500	✓	
Rent received	500		✓

218 GAS ERROR

Account name	Amount £	Debit ✓	Credit ✓
Gas expenses	300	✓	
Electricity expenses	300		✓

219 BUILDING ERROR

Account name	Amount £	Debit ✓	Credit ✓
Suspense	360,000	✓	
Bank	360,000		✓

220 SALES ERROR

Account name	Amount £	Debit ✓	Credit ✓
Sales	2,000	✓	
VAT	2,000		✓

221 MOTOR ERROR

Account name	Amount £	Debit ✓	Credit ✓
Motor expenses	700	✓	
Motor vehicles	700		✓

222 INVENTORY ERROR

Account name	Amount £	Debit ✓	Credit ✓
Purchases	375	✓	
VAT	75	✓	
Payables ledger control	450		✓

223 SUBSCRIPTIONS ERROR

Account name	Amount £	Debit ✓	Credit ✓
Subscriptions expense	160	✓	
Bank	160		✓

224 PURCHASE ERROR

Account name	Amount £	Debit ✓	Credit ✓
VAT	1,500	✓	
Purchases	1,500		✓

225 INSURANCE ERROR

Account name	Amount £	Debit ✓	Credit ✓
Payables ledger control	2,700	✓	
Bank	2,700		✓

KAPLAN PUBLISHING

226 CB INTERIORS

(i)

Account name	Amount £	Debit ✓	Credit ✓
Payables ledger control	960	✓	

(ii)

Account name	Amount £	Debit ✓	Credit ✓
Payables ledger control	9,600		✓

(iii)

Account name	Amount £	Debit ✓	Credit ✓
Suspense	8,640	✓	

227 ROGER DODGER

(i)

Account name	Amount £	Debit ✓	Credit ✓
VAT	1,680	✓	

(ii)

Account name	Amount £	Debit ✓	Credit ✓
VAT	1,320		✓

(iii)

Account name	Amount £	Debit ✓	Credit ✓
Suspense	360		✓

228 A CUT ABOVE

(i)

Account name	Amount £	Debit ✓	Credit ✓
Payables ledger control	6,182		✓

(ii)

Account name	Amount £	Debit ✓	Credit ✓
Payables ledger control	5,952	✓	

(iii)

Account name	Amount £	Debit ✓	Credit ✓
Suspense	230	✓	

229 RESTCO

(i)

Account name	Amount £	Debit ✓	Credit ✓
Sales	8,080	✓	

(ii)

Account name	Amount £	Debit ✓	Credit ✓
Sales	8,800		✓

(iii)

Account name	Amount £	Debit ✓	Credit ✓
Suspense	720	✓	

230 JOHNNY JOINER

(a)

Account name	Amount £	Debit ✓	Credit ✓
Suspense	14,363		✓

(b)

Account name	Amount £	Debit ✓	Credit ✓
Suspense	14,363	✓	
Sales	14,363		✓

231 BUCKLEY DRAINS

(a)

Account name	Amount £	Debit ✓	Credit ✓
Suspense	10,805		✓

(b)

Account name	Amount £	Debit ✓	Credit ✓
Suspense	10,805	✓	
Payables ledger control	10,805		✓

(c)   Show one reason for maintaining the journal

	✓
To correct errors only	
To correct errors and record transactions that have not been recorded in any other book of prime entry	✓
To record transactions from every other book of prime entry.	

232 MENDONCA

(a)

Account name	Amount £	Debit ✓	Credit ✓
Suspense	1,980		✓

(b)

Account name	Amount £	Debit ✓	Credit ✓
Suspense	1,980	✓	
Wages	900	✓	
Bank	2,880		✓

233 BEASANT

(a)

Account name	Amount £	Debit ✓	Credit ✓
Suspense	15,000		✓

(b)

Account name	Amount £	Debit ✓	Credit ✓
Suspense	15,000	✓	
Sales	12,500		✓
VAT	2,500		✓

(c)   **Show one reason for maintaining the journal**

	✓
To detect fraud	
To record non-regular transactions	✓
To record goods sold on credit	

234 PAT'S CAFE

(a)   **What entry would be made in the suspense account to balance the trial balance?**

Account name	Amount £	Debit ✓	Credit ✓
Suspense	4,650	✓	

(b)

Account name	Balance £	Debit ✓	Credit ✓
Bank interest paid	235	✓	
Bank interest received	61		✓
Insurance	550	✓	
Motor vehicles	6500	✓	

235 TWINKLE'S TRINKETS

(a)

Account name	Amount £	Debit ✓	Credit ✓
Suspense	776		✓

(b)

Account name	Balance £	Debit ✓	Credit ✓
Motor expenses	8,744	✓	
Repairs and renewals	1,210	✓	
Rent payable	3,700	✓	
Rent received	1,700		✓

236 SPARKS AND MENCER

Account name	Balance £	Debit ✓	Credit ✓
Heat and light	655	✓	
Rates	1,416	✓	
Loan interest expense	165	✓	
Rent received	119		✓

Section 7

MOCK ASSESSMENT QUESTIONS

TIME = 2 HOURS

TASK 1 (10 marks)

This task is about different business types and their functions.

(a) **Identify the correct business type described in each of the statements below. There may be more than one type relevant to each statement.** (4 marks)

	Sole trader ✓	Partner ✓	Limited company ✓
A business owned and operated by one person			
A business that must be incorporated			
Must register for corporation tax with HMRC.			
They will need to register with HMRC for self-assessment of income tax.			

(b) **Indicate which of the following entities have limited liability or unlimited liability.** (3 marks)

	Limited liability ✓	Unlimited liability ✓
A business owned and operated by one person		
A business managed by directors		
A business owned and operated by two or more people		

(c)   Identify which functions of the business match the description from the picklist below.

(3 marks)

	Function ✓
Concerned with all aspects of recruitment, selection, training and development of employees.	
Concerned with the acquisition of raw materials, their conversion into finished products and the supply of that finished product to the customer.	
Concerned with the promotion and selling of products and services, including market research and advertising activities.	

Picklist: Finance, Operations, Marketing, Human resources, Distribution

TASK 2   (13 marks)

This task is about the finance function, its information requirements and sources, and its role within the wider organisation.

(a)   **Identify TWO of the characteristics of useful information from the list below.**

(2 marks)

A   Costly – useful information is always expensive to collate

B   Consistent – in both the basis of calculation or estimation and in the presentation of that information

C   Quick – Information should be available immediately

D   Comparable – to make meaningful comparison of equivalent information

(b)   **Identify whether the following statements about the role of information within the finance function are true or false.**   (3 marks)

Written communication must always be formal   – True/False

Primary data is normally collected for a specific purpose   – True/False

The information produced by the finance function will help managers of the business make better decisions.   – True/False

(c)   **Identify TWO responsibilities that the finance function has to external stakeholders.**

(2 marks)

A   Producing the statutory financial statements

B   Producing information to assist and support other parts of the business

C   Producing management accounts and supporting information

D   Producing and filing other returns and documents required by law

Your hours of work are 8am to 4.30pm with an hour for lunch each day. Your manager has suggested that you attend college and has asked you to take a look at your work schedule to identify the best day for this. The work schedule below details the days when routine tasks must be completed and the amount of time each task takes to complete.

Task Description	Day	Duration	Frequency
Answer emails	Daily	1 hour	Twice daily
Process sales invoices	Tuesday & Friday	2 hours	Twice weekly
Process purchase invoices	Monday & Thursday	3 hours	Twice weekly
Prepare reports	Monday	1 hour	Weekly
Reconcile statements	Friday	1 hour	Weekly
Team meeting	Wednesday	1 hour	Weekly

(d) **Identify on which day you will be busiest with routine tasks and the number of hours spent.**

(2 marks)

Picklist:

Monday/Tuesday/Wednesday/Thursday/Friday/Saturday/Sunday

3 hrs/ 4 hrs/ 5 hrs/ 6 hrs/ 7hrs

(e) **Identify which day would be best for attending college, based on your workload.** **(1 mark)**

Picklist:

Monday/Tuesday/Wednesday/Thursday/Friday/Saturday/Sunday

(f) You have received an email from a colleague in the sales department and they need details of a customer's credit limit before they can continue with the sale. There is a company policy to ensure this is checked before large orders are placed.

Which is the most effective way to respond to this request? **(1 mark)**

A   Send a letter by first class post

B   Respond by email

C   Ask another member of the team to tell them for you, you are busy after all

D   Call a meeting with your manager and the sales manager to discuss the policy

(g) **Which of the following TWO would ensure and improve the financial solvency of the business?** **(2 marks)**

A   Pay dividends to keep shareholders happy increasing the overdraft or borrowing the funds if needed

B   Delay payments which are not essential, such as the purchase of non-current assets or dividend payments.

C   Pay suppliers before they are due and increase Inventory

D   Credit control measures put in place to reduce the risk of bad debts and ensure timely receipt of monies

TASK 3 (14 marks)

This task is about corporate social responsibility (CSR), ethics and sustainability.

(a) **Identify whether each of the following statements relating to sustainability is TRUE or FALSE.** (3 marks)

	True	False
Sustainability involves taking a long-term view and allowing the needs of present generations to be met without compromising the ability of future generations to meet their own needs.		
Sustainability involves considering the needs of the organisation's shareholders only.		
Accountants have a public interest duty to protect society as a whole and the organisation's sustainability.		

(b) **Which of the following concepts does NOT form part of the 'triple bottom line' principle that encourages sustainability?** (1 mark)

A   Planet

B   Place

C   Profit

D   Planet

(c) Your boss has told you that there are going to be some redundancies in the company. You will not be affected, but she has named a number of people who will be, including a good friend of yours who is in the process of buying a holiday home in Cornwall. You know that your friend would not be able to afford the property if she were to lose her job and that she would pull out of the purchase if she knew about the redundancy plans.

The news of the redundancies will not be made public for several weeks.

Indicate your best course of action. Select ONE answer only. (1 mark)

From an ethical point of view you should tell your friend about the redundancies on the grounds it could save her unnecessary financial problems and distress.	
You should not tell your friend about the redundancies.	

(d) You have been asked to complete the bank reconciliation for the week. However, you have other tasks to do and will not have enough time complete the work properly.

Indicate which fundamental ethical principle is under threat. (1 mark)

Integrity	
Confidentiality	
Professional competence and due care	
Professional behaviour	
Objectivity	

(e) **(i)** You have been asked by your manager to calculate depreciation on motor vehicles for the year, and then to reduce the calculated amount by 10% to reduce the expense and increase profit for the year.

Complete the following sentence using the picklist below. **(1 mark)**

This is a threat to the principle _____.

Picklist:

professional competence and due care

professional behaviour

objectivity

integrity

confidentiality

(ii) **Identify TWO actions you should take from the following list.** **(2 marks)**

Speak to the finance director directly.

Prepare the adjustments for your manager as they told you to do it

Seek advice from the AAT.

Speak to your friends and see what they think you should do.

(f) **Identify the statement that best describes the AAT Code of Professional Ethics.** **(1 mark)**

A It is based on law and must be followed for members to do the right thing.

B It is a set of principles that guides members to do the right thing.

C It is a set of rules that must be complied with.

(g) **Match the principle with each of the statements below.** **(5 marks)**

Statement	Integrity ✓	Objectivity ✓	Professional behaviour ✓	Professional competence ✓	Confidentiality ✓
You should not allow bias, conflict of interest or undue influence of others to override your professional or business judgements.					
You should act diligently and in accordance with applicable technical and professional standards					

You should be straightforward and honest in the performance of your work duties and responsibilities.					
Do not disclose any such information to third parties without proper and specific authority, unless there is a legal or professional right or duty to disclose.					
You should comply with relevant laws and regulations and avoid any action that could bring you or your profession into disrepute.					

TASK 4 (22 marks)

This task is about processing bookkeeping transactions and communicating information.

You have received the invoice below from a credit supplier. The supplier has agreed to allow a 10% bulk discount off the list price of £0.75 per item.

Dawson Ltd

11 Hove Street, Grangeton, GX11 4HB

VAT Registration No. 398 4673 00

Invoice No. D1672

To: SCM Products   15 May 20XX
      14 London Road
      Parton, PA21 7NL

                                    £
1,200 ... Product D92 @ £0.75 each   900.00
VAT @ 20%   180.00

                                  1,080.00

Terms of payment: Net monthly account

You notice that the invoice amounts are incorrect.

(a) **What should be the correct amounts of the invoice?** (3 marks)

Net £	VAT £	Total £

You have received another invoice from the same supplier whose account code is DAW32. There was no bulk discount offered for this order but the supplier has offered a prompt payment discount. You are ready to enter this invoice into the appropriate daybook

---

Dawson Ltd

11 Hove Street, Grangeton, GX11 4HB

VAT Registration No. 398 4673 00

Invoice No. D1676

To: SCM Products   17 May 20XX
      14 London Road
      Parton, PA21 7NL

                                                              £
250 ... Product D87 @ £0.62 each   155.00
VAT @ 20%   31.00
                                                        _____

                                                         186.00
                                                        _____

Terms of payment: 3% discount for payment within 10 days of date of invoice

---

(b) **Complete the entries in the daybook below by:**

- **selecting the correct daybook title, and**

- **making the necessary entries.** (9 marks)

Title	▽

▽ Drop down list for task 1.3 (b):

Discounts allowed daybook
Discounts received daybook
Purchases daybook
Purchases returns daybook
Sales daybook
Sales returns daybook

Date 20XX	Details	Supplier account code	Invoice number	Total £	VAT £	Net £	Product D87	Product D92
	▽	▽						

∇ Drop down list for task 1.3 (b):

Details

Dawson Ltd
SCM Products

Supplier account code

DAW32
D1672
D1676

You must now prepare a payment to the supplier for invoice D1676 in order to take advantage of the prompt payment discount offered.

(c)   **What will be the amount paid and what is the latest date by which the supplier should receive payment?**   **(2 marks)**

Amount to be paid £	Date by which payment should be received
	∇

∇ Drop down list for task 1.3 (c):

15 May 20XX
17 May 20XX
25 May 20XX
27 May 20XX
31 May 20XX
30 June 20XX

You now need to deal with the note below which you have received from your line manager, Orla Green.

Note

We have overpaid an invoice for £1,248 from a credit supplier. Further information is below.
Supplier: Parton Painters
Invoice number 612, dated 12 May 20XX
Payment cheque for £1,428 sent to the supplier on 10 June 20XX
Please send an email from yourself, an accounts assistant, to Janice Frost at Parton Painters. You should explain the situation, specify the amount of the overpayment, and request a payment to correct the error.
Thanks
Orla

(d) **Prepare an appropriate business email to Parton Painters, making sure that you include all relevant information.** **(6 marks)**

To: jfrost@partonpainters.co.uk

From: accounts@scmproducts.co.uk

Subject

A return needs to be processed to a credit supplier for £240 including VAT.

(e) **What day book would the return be recorded in?** **(1 mark)**

Title	▽

▽ Drop down list for task 1.3 (e):

Discounts allowed daybook
Discounts received daybook
Purchases daybook
Purchases returns daybook
Sales daybook
Sales returns daybook

(f) **What impact would the return to the credit supplier have on profit?** **(1 mark)**

A return processed to a credit supplier for £240 including VAT would cause profit to be

	▽

▽ Drop down list for task 1.3 (f):

higher
lower

TASK 5 (10 marks)

This task is about control accounts, reconciliations and using journals to correct errors.

You have received the bank statement for June and are checking it against the cash book.

Bank statement

Date 20XX	Details	Paid out £	Paid in £	Balance £
01 Jun	Balance b/f			791 C
04 Jun	Counter credit		1,573	2,365 C
07 Jun	Cheque 015263	605		1,759 C
16 Jun	Cheque 015265	1,428		331 C
20 Jun	Cheque 015249	387		56 D
24 Jun	Cheque 015267	211		267 D
27 Jun	Counter credit		1,195	928 C
28 Jun	Cheque 015266	509		419 C
D = Debit C = Credit				

Cash book

Date 20XX	Details	Bank £	Date 20XX	Cheque number	Details	Bank £
01 Jun	Balance b/f	404	03 Jun	015263	Amy Cox	605
04 Jun	QP Ltd	1,573	05 Jun	015264	Hal James	753
20 Jun	Koyt plc	844	10 Jun	015265	Parton Painters	1,428
27 Jun	Freya Rose	1,195	18 Jun	015266	Sal Ltd	509
			20 Jun	015267	Tay Traders	211

(a) **Identify which item has caused the difference in the opening balances.** (1 mark)

Reason	
An unpresented cheque for £387	☐
An outstanding lodgement for £387	☐
An unpresented cheque for £1,195	☐
An outstanding lodgement for £1,195	☐

Having identified that there are no additional transactions to be recorded in the cash book you are now ready to total and balance the cash book.

(b) **What will be the cash book balance carried down?** **(1 mark)**

Amount £	Debit	Credit
	☐	☐

(c) **What will be the total of each of the cash book debit and credit columns after you have recorded the balance carried down that you calculated in (b)?** **(1 mark)**

Amount £

Your next task is to check that the cash book balance reconciles with the bank statement.

(d) **Complete the bank reconciliation statement at 30 June.** **(3 marks)**

Bank reconciliation statement		£
Balance as per bank statement		
Add:		
	∇	
Less		
	∇	
Balance as per cash book		

∇ Drop down list for task 4 (b):

Amy Cox
Cheque 015249
Counter credit
Freya Rose
Hal James
Koyt plc
Parton Painters
QP Ltd
Sal Ltd
Tay Traders

You have now completed and totalled the trial balance, but find it does not balance. The credit column is £270 more than the debit column so you have opened a suspense account.

(e) Will the opening balance in the suspense account be a debit or credit entry? (1 mark)

Debit ☐

Credit ☐

You have identified that the error in the trial balance has arisen from a bank payment of £636 for a rail fare being recorded in the travel account as £366. The entry in the bank account was correct.

You have partially prepared journal entries to correct the error and clear the suspense account.

(f) Complete each journal entry by inserting the appropriate amount in either the debit or credit column. Do NOT enter a zero in unused debit or credit column cells. (3 marks)

Journal to remove the incorrect entry

Account name	Debit £	Credit £
Travel		

Journal to record the correct entry

Account name	Debit £	Credit £
Travel		

Journal to clear the suspense account

Account name	Debit £	Credit £
Suspense		

TASK 6 (7 marks)

This task is about the principles of contract law.

(a)   **Identify which of the following courts would not be used for a civil law case.   (1 mark)**

	✓
Supreme Court	
High Court	
Magistrates Court	
Crown Court	

The following information will be needed for parts (b) to (d)

Ali is an antique dealer and one Saturday in November 20X7 he put a vase in the window of his shop with a sign which stated 'exceptional piece of 19th century pottery – on offer for £500'.

Ben happened to notice the vase as he walked past the shop and thought he would like to have it. Unfortunately, as he was late for an important meeting, he could not go into the shop to buy it, but as soon as his meeting was finished he wrote to Ali agreeing to buy the vase for the stated price of £500. The letter was posted at 11:30 am.

Just before closing time at 5 pm. Di came into Ali's shop and she also offered £400 for the vase. This time Ali agreed to sell the vase at that price and Di promised to return the following Monday with the money.

On the Monday morning Ali received the letter from Ben before Di could arrive to pay and collect the vase.

(b)   **Identify whether the following statements regarding an offer are true or false.   (2 marks)**

	True	False
An offer must be in writing.		
An offer must be communicated to the offeree.		

(c)   **Identify whether the following statements are true or false.   (2 marks)**

	True	False
The shop window sign and display is an offer.		
Ben's letter to Ali is an offer.		

(d)   **Identify whether the following statements are true or false.   (2 marks)**

	True	False
There is a contract between Ali and Ben.		
There is no contract between Ali and Di.		

TASK 7 (10 marks)

This task is about bookkeeping systems, receipts and payments, and the importance of information and data security.

You work for a company that produces gift boxes that they sell online, currently the accounting system is installed on each desktop computer and backed up each night onto a server. Your manager would like to change the system to a cloud-based accounting system and has asked you to produce some notes that he can present to the directors.

(a) **(i)** State THREE ways in which the use of a cloud-based accounting system could be advantageous to the company. (3 marks)

(ii) State THREE concerns the directors may need to be aware of, in regards to using a cloud- based accounting system in the company. (3 marks)

(b) Your company has recently had a security breach and access was obtained into the system. On investigation it came to light that a member of staff was using the password 1234 and access was via their laptop.

Your manager has asked you to send some notes that can be forwarded to the employees to remind them of password security rules.

Give FOUR suggestions to help remind users about password security. **(4 marks)**

TASK 8 (14 marks)

This task is about the external business environment.

(a) **(i)** **Which ONE of the following best describes the concept of 'complementary goods'?** **(1 mark)**

A   The purchase of one good means that a similar good is not purchased

B   A number of goods exist, any of which can be purchased to satisfy a need

C   One good is free and the other has to be paid for

D   The purchase of one good leads to the purchase of another

(ii) **Which ONE of the following would explain a rise in the price of a good accompanied by a fall in the quantity sold?** **(1 mark)**

A   A decrease in supply

B   An increase in demand

C   A decrease in demand

D   An increase in supply

(iii) **Complete the following statements using the pick list below.** **(2 marks)**

_____is the study of the economic behaviour of individual consumers, firms and industries. It focuses on how these three individual parts of an economy make decisions about how to allocate scarce resources.

_____is the use of government spending and/or taxation as a tool to influence the economy.

Picklist: Macroeconomics, Demand, Microeconomics, Economy, Fiscal policy, Supply

(b) You're planning on going on holiday to Turkey. The value of the pound sterling has increased against the Turkish Lira.

Select TWO statements from below that describes how this will impact the cost of you buying goods and services when you are there. **(2 marks)**

A depreciation of the pound sterling against the Turkish Lira means that you will be able to purchase more Turkish Lira for a pound.

An appreciation of the pound sterling against the Turkish Lira means that you will be able to purchase more Turkish Lira for a pound.

This will result in the pound sterling cost of goods and services you buy in Turkey being cheaper.

This will result in the pound sterling cost of goods and services you buy in Turkey being more expensive.

(c) **Identify which ONE of the following situations is likely to cause an increase in demand.** **(1 mark)**

A cheaper substitute available

Retail Price index rises

Reduction in the price of the good

(d) **Identify whether the following risks to a business are internal or external.** **(4 marks)**

	Internal	External
New competitors in the market place		
Loss of key staff to a competitor		
Machine stoppage due to power failure		
Regulations imposed by the government on the industry		

(e) **Which one of the following sentences best describes risk?** **(1 mark)**

A   The exposure to the adverse consequences of dangerous environments

B   The expected impact of uncertain future events on objectives

C   The chance of being caught doing something unethical

D   The impact of the exposure to the adverse consequences of uncertain future events

AJ Limited have recently signed a contract with a company in Switzerland, who use currency known as the Swiss Franc (CHF). The exchange rate has changed from £1 = 4.5CHF to £1 = 4.2CHF

(f) **(i)** **Identify the statement which explains what has happened.** **(1 mark)**

The pound has appreciated against the Swiss Franc.

The pound has strengthened against the Swiss Franc.

The pound has depreciated against the Swiss Franc.

Section 8

MOCK ASSESSMENT ANSWERS

TASK 1

(a)

	Sole Trader ✓	Partner ✓	Limited company ✓
A business owned and operated by one person	✓		
A business that must be incorporated			✓
Must register for corporation tax with HMRC.			✓
They will need to register with HMRC for self-assessment of income tax.	✓		

(b)

	Limited liability ✓	Unlimited liability ✓
A business owned and operated by one person		✓
A business managed by directors	✓	
A business owned and operated by two or more people		✓

(c)

	Function ✓
Concerned with all aspects of recruitment, selection, training and development of employees.	Human resources
Concerned with the acquisition of raw materials, their conversion into finished products and the supply of that finished product to the customer.	Operations
Concerned with the promotion and selling of products and services, including market research and advertising activities.	Marketing

TASK 2

(a)   B   Consistent – in both the basis of calculation or estimation and in the presentation of that information

        D   Comparable – to make meaningful comparison of equivalent information

(b)   Written communication must always be formal   – False

       Primary data is normally collected for a specific purpose   – True

       The information produced by the finance function will help managers of the business make better decisions.   – True

(c)   A   Producing the statutory financial statements

        D   Producing and filing other returns and documents required by law

(d)   Monday, 5 hrs

(e)   Wednesday

(f)   B   Respond by email

(g)   B   Delay payments which are not essential, such as the purchase of non-current assets or dividend payments.

        D   Credit control measures put in place to reduce the risk of bad debts and ensure timely receipt of monies.

TASK 3

(a)

	True	False
Sustainability involves taking a long-term view and allowing the needs of present generations to be met without compromising the ability of future generations to meet their own needs.	✓	
Sustainability involves considering the needs of the organisation's shareholders only.		✓
Accountants have a public interest duty to protect society as a whole and the organisation's sustainability.	✓	

(b)   B   Place

(c)

From an ethical point of view you should tell your friend about the redundancies on the grounds it could save her unnecessary financial problems and distress.	
You should not tell your friend about the redundancies	✓
	You should not tell your friend about the redundancies as to do so would breach confidentiality.

(d)

Integrity	
Confidentiality	
Professional competence and due care	✓
Professional behaviour	
Objectivity	

(e)   **(i)**   This is a threat to the principle **integrity**.

 (ii)   Speak to the finance director directly.

 Seek advice from the AAT.

(f)   B   It is a set of principles that guides members to do the right thing.

(g)

Statement	Integrity ✓	Objectivity ✓	Professional behaviour ✓	Professional competence ✓	Confidentiality ✓
You should not allow bias, conflict of interest or undue influence of others to override your professional or business judgements.		✓			
You should act diligently and in accordance with applicable technical and professional standards				✓	
You should be straightforward and honest in the performance of your work duties and responsibilities.	✓				
Do not disclose any such information to third parties without proper and specific authority, unless there is a legal or professional right or duty to disclose.					✓
You should comply with relevant laws and regulations and avoid any action that could bring you or your profession into disrepute.			✓		

TASK 4

(a)

Net £	VAT £	Total £
810	162	972

(b)

Title	Purchases daybook ▽

Date 20XX	Details	Supplier account code	Invoice number	Total £	VAT £	Net £	Product D87	Product D92
17 May	Dawson Ltd ▽	DAW32 ▽	D1676	186	31	155	155	

(c)

Amount to be paid £	Date by which payment should be received
180.42	27 May 20XX ▽

(d)

To: jfrost@partonpainters.co.uk

From: accounts@scmproducts.co.uk

Subject Incorrect payment

Hello Janice

On 10 June 20XX we sent you a cheque for £1,428 in payment of your invoice 612 dated 12 May 20XX.

We have now realised that the amount of the cheque was incorrect, it should have been £1,248 which is the amount of your invoice.

As a result, we have overpaid by £180 so we would appreciate it if you could send us a payment for the amount of the overpayment.

Kind regards

Accounts Assistant

(e)

Title	Purchases returns daybook ▽

(f)

A return processed to a credit supplier for £240 including VAT would cause profit to be

higher ▽

TASK 5

(a)

Reason	
An unpresented cheque for £387	✓
An outstanding lodgement for £387	☐
An unpresented cheque for £1,195	☐
An outstanding lodgement for £1,195	☐

(b)

Amount £	Debit	Credit
510	☐	✓

(c)

Amount £
4,016

(d)

Bank reconciliation statement		£
Balance as per bank statement		419
Add:		
Koyt plc	∇	844
Less		
Hal James	∇	753
Balance as per cash book		510

(e)

Debit ✓

Credit ☐

(f) **Journal to remove the incorrect entry**

Account name	Debit £	Credit £
Travel		366

Journal to record the correct entry

Account name	Debit £	Credit £
Travel	636	

Journal to clear the suspense account

Account name	Debit £	Credit £
Suspense		270

TASK 6

(a)

	✓
Supreme Court	
High Court	
Magistrates Court	
Crown Court	✓

(b)

	True	False
An offer must be in writing.		✓
An offer must be communicated to the offeree.	✓	

(c)

	True	False
The shop window sign and display is an offer.		✓
Ben's letter to Ali is an offer.	✓	

(d)

	True	False
There is a contract between Ali and Ben.		✓
There is no contract between Ali and Di.		✓

TASK 7

(a) **(i)** **1 mark per relevant point up to 3 marks**

- the ability to access data anywhere and at any time from multiple locations

- access to real-time information, rather than having to wait for processing and output

- always using the latest version of software

- the functionality to use analytical tools, either within the cloud accounting itself, or provided via third party apps and tools

- the ability to grant secure access to data and information to trusted third parties e.g. the organisation's auditor or financial advisor

- connection to bank accounts to enable payments to be made e.g. periodic VAT payments, or to enable customers to pay for goods and services.

(ii) **1 mark per relevant point up to 3 marks**

- reliance upon the internet and the speed of recording and transmitting data and information

- lack of customisation software so that only 'standard' packages are available which may not precisely meet the needs of the organisation

- lack of data security, particularly if it contains information that is regarded as confidemntial or sensitive, such as the personal details of customers and bank account information

- 'lock-in' to one system which may prevent or deter transfer to another provider of cloud accounting services.

(b) **1 mark per relevant point up to 4 marks**

- It must not be written down.

- It must not be possible to guess the password easily, such as the use of names, motor vehicle licence numbers, birth dates or the like.

- The password should consist of at least one non-letter character (special character or number) and have at least six characters. The selection of trivial passwords (BBBBBB, 123456) must be prevented.

- Preset passwords (e.g. set by the manufacturer at the time of delivery) must be replaced by individually selected, unique passwords as soon as possible.

- The password must be kept secret and should be known only to the authorised user.

- The password must be changed regularly, e.g. every 90 days. This will ensure that if an unauthorised person has obtained it, he or she will have limited use.

- The password should be altered if it has, or may have, come to the knowledge of unauthorised persons.

- After any alteration of the password, previous passwords should no longer be used and re-use of previous passwords should be prevented by the IT system.

TASK 8

(a) **(i)** D The purchase of one good leads to the purchase of another

(ii) A A decrease in supply

(iii) **Microeconomics** is the study of the economic behaviour of individual consumers, firms and industries. It focuses on how these three individual parts of an economy make decisions about how to allocate scarce resources.

Fiscal policy is the use of government spending and/or taxation as a tool to influence the economy.

(b) An appreciation of the pound sterling against the Turkish Lira means that you will be able to purchase more Turkish Lira for a pound.

This will result in the pound sterling cost of goods and services you buy in Turkey being cheaper.

(c) Reduction in the price of the good

(d)

	Internal	External
New competitors in the market place		✓
Loss of key staff to a competitor	✓	
Machine stoppage due to power failure	✓	
Regulations imposed by the government on the industry		✓

(e) B The expected impact of uncertain future events on objectives

(f) **(i)** The pound has depreciated against the Swiss Franc.

(ii) Imports from Switzerland will cost more.